THE SOUTH WALES TRANSPORT COMPANY LTD

100th ANNIVERSARY

by Vernon Morgan

SWT 100

Published by Vernon Morgan
February 2014.
Designed by – Proprint, Carmarthen.
Printed in Wales by – Proprint, Carmarthen.

ISBN 978-0-9574045-1-9

All photographs are from the author's collection
unless otherwise stated.

All rights reserved. No part of this book may be reproduced or transmitted in any form or by any means electronic or mechanical, including photocopying, recording or by any information storage and retrieval system without permission from the publisher in writing.

© Copyright Vernon Morgan (2014).

Photographs:-
Cover picture: The South Wales Transport Company Ltd., was regarded as one of AEC's most loyal customers. During the company's existence, well over 1,000 AEC's had been operated, ranging from early YC's to later Reliance's and 'S' types to Bridgemaster's. Most types and models were tried over a period of 67 years. Pictured here is 282 DWN (38), one of the eight unique Roe bodied AEC Regent V's which were once operated by the company. These buses were specially built to operate services beneath exceptionally low bridges in the New Dock district of Llanelli, one bridge having a clearance of just 9 feet. It can now be seen in pristine condition at the Swansea Bus Museum, and is used for open day events.

Vernon Morgan.

Title page: One of the first vehicles acquired by the company was this 1914 Milnes-Daimler 30 hp double decker, registered L 1128. It was one of two acquired with the business of F.L.Lewis, Pontardawe in 1914.

Rear cover (upper): South Wales Transport acquired the well-established business of AE & FR Brewer, Caerau, in January 1988. The Brewers name however continued to be used as a subsidiary company for a further 11 years, and absorbed the Llynfi undertaking at Maesteg. The Brewers livery was changed from its original blue, turquoise and white to red white and yellow in 1992, as seen here on AWN 812V (812), a Leyland National Mk l transferred from the main SWT fleet.

Byron Gage.

Rear cover (lower): This livery of leaf green and lime green, with red and yellow relief was introduced on conventional vehicles from April 1987 onwards. ECW bodied Bristol VRT, BEP 974V (974) was one of the first VRT's to receive the new livery, and is captured here entering Swansea's Quadrant bus station on 21st July, 1987.

Vernon Morgan.

CONTENTS

AUTHORS ACKNOWLEDGEMENTS

I would like to take this opportunity to thank numerous people for their sincere help and assistance in compiling this book which took over two years.

First of all I would like to thank my daughter Katie for her contribution in the production of this book, scanning and embedding each photograph, and correcting small grammatical errors. Also to Kath, my wife, for her co-operation and understanding, correcting my spelling and proof reading my notes.

Special thanks are due to the late Chris Taylor, transport historian, for his contribution of historical notes, and to Steve Powell, John Jones, Byron Gage, Paul Fox, Tony Wade, Phil Connor and staff at First Cymru Buses, and to the late Roy Marshall, for their contributions of photographs and historical material. Most other photographs are views taken by myself or views from my large collection, which are the copyright of persons unknown as they are not back stamped. No discourtesy to the photographer is intended through lack of acknowledgement, in view of which I trust they will accept my sincere thanks.

Finally, I would like to thank the staff at Proprint, Carmarthen for their professional assistance in producing the final product.

INTRODUCTION

Public transport is the life-line of civilisation. Its meteoric development in the late 19th century is the most spectacular chain of events in the industrial history of man. From the horse-drawn coach and covered wagon, to jet aircraft and the modern omnibus, the span of time was less than a hundred years.

The history of public transport in South Wales is a very complex one that began during the horse drawn mail-coach days of the 18th century, changing to the railroad and later to the mechanical mode of transport.

This publication, illustrated with views from throughout the company's operational area, has been published to commemorate the 100th anniversary of the inauguration of 'The South Wales Transport Company Ltd,' in 1914. South Wales Transport was a subsidiary of the privately owned British Electric Traction Company Ltd, (BET), a company that was already operating the Swansea tramway system, known as the Swansea Improvements and Tramways Company.

The South Wales Transport Company Ltd., continued to be a BET group subsidiary until 1967, when all the bus operating interests of BET passed to the Transport Holding Company (THC), a state owned concern, and in 1969, South Wales Transport inevitably became part of the state owned National Bus Company (NBC).

Under a Tory Government in 1986, a new era of competition began as a result of the 1985 Transport Act. This act also provided for the privatisation of NBC, resulting in a management buy-out of SWT in May 1987. Three years later, SWT was sold to Badgerline Holdings retaining the South Wales Transport name. On 16th June, 1995, Badgerline Holdings merged with Grampian Regional Transport and formed First Bus PLC with a fleet of 5,600 vehicles, yet the South Wales Transport Company name continued to be used.

The name was finally phased out in April 1998 in favour of 'First Cymru', a regional name for First Bus PLC, but the vehicle legal lettering still remained as 'South Wales Transport' until 28th March, 1999. The South Wales Transport Company's operator licence discs, PG 421 continued to be used until 31st May, 1999, which was consequently the final demise of the SWT name. However, the 'O' licence disc number PG 0000421 continued - as 'First Cymru Buses Ltd', and is still currently operational.

It is interesting to note that in 1994, the South Wales Transport group (Badgerline) was by far the largest bus operator in Wales. Having absorbed numerous companies throughout the years, there were no less than 168 companies involved in the structure of the company, so to conclude, a South Wales Transport family tree has been incorporated into this 100th anniversary publication.

IN THE BEGINNING

Although we are now celebrating the one hundredth anniversary since the inauguration of The South Wales Transport Company Limited in 1914, we must, to get the story in its proper perspective, go back as far as 1874 when the first horse drawn trams appeared on the streets of Swansea. Since that time, Swansea has been faithfully served by a forward looking and progressive public transport system which, without doubt, must rank as second-to-none with any city of comparable size.`

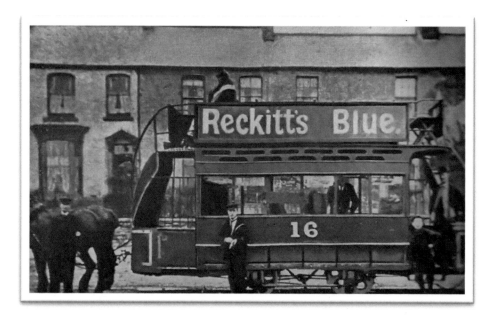

A Swansea horse drawn tram circa 1900.

The first major change came in 1898, when the British Electric Traction Company Limited took over the running of the Swansea tramway system, and through the Swansea Improvements and Tramways Company Limited, set about discarding the horse drawn trams for the electrically operated type. By 1900, the change was completed and Swansea became the first town in Wales to have electric tramways. Within the confines of Swansea's boundary, Ynysforgan, Sketty and Port Tennant, the tramway service may have been adequate at that time, but it was becoming increasingly obvious that a means of road transport for the public between Swansea, and it's out-lying districts, was necessary. It was economically and geographically impossible to extend the tramways to many of the districts but already mechanically propelled vehicles were making their presence felt and of course in this system was the solution to the problem. The visionaries of those days were quick to see the adaptability of the mechanically driven vehicle and the advantage of its mobility. However, the idea was not to compete with the tramway system, but to act as feeders to it. It was this idea which led to the formation of The South Wales Transport Company Limited on 10th February, 1914, and by May of that year, Swansea saw its first motor omnibus.

To house its buses, The South Wales Transport Company acquired premises in Brunswick Street, Swansea, which they shared with a builders' merchant for a time before eventually buying the whole premises of 7,549 square yards at a cost of £7,176. It was here, also, that the company established its head office. The original head office had been Rutland Street, Swansea, headquarters of the Swansea Improvements & Tramways Company, (S.I.T.C.). Brunswick Street depot was capable of housing 97 vehicles.

On the 2nd May 1914, the first service was operated. This was between Ynysforgan and Ynysmeudwy, near Pontardawe in the Swansea Valley. The service was further extended into the Swansea Valley by the acquisition of F. L. Lewis Limited of Pontardawe, who operated a bus service between Ynysforgan and Ystalyfera. Mr F.L. Lewis was later to become the Engineer and Manager of The South Wales Transport Co. Incidentally, the Swansea Valley service was listed in the company's publications as service No. 1. Likewise, the second service which was introduced on 11th July 1914, and operated between Cwmbwrla and Llanelli was known as service No. 2. This service was extended into the centre of Swansea by the acquisition of Thomas Jones, Gorseinon. By 25th August 1914, service No. 3, Morriston to Taibach (Port Talbot), and No.4, Swansea to Mumbles, were also in operation. Many of the operating staff, of course, came from ready trained men of the Tramways Company who had volunteered for transfer. Also taken over in May 1914, was the horse-bus business of Moses Lee and Son, who ran 'unlicensed' between Swansea and Mumbles, and in 1915 the business of T. Evans & Sons, Fforestfach was acquired with his 3 vehicles and a service Swansea to Gorseinon via Fforestfach. Acquiring Evans' business secured the company's position on the Llanelli route.

As can be judged the new company was quickly establishing itself, but unfortunately, the storm clouds of the 1st World War had broken and buses as well as crews were called upon to serve the country in its time of need. A large proportion of the buses owned by the company were impressed for military service, and naturally, any further extension of its activities was out of the question, except where it was to help in the war effort. In this connection the records show an introduction of a service between Llanelli and Pembrey munitions factory in 1915, and in 1916 a service to operate between Swansea and Gowerton steelworks.

Similar ventures were tried in south-east Wales, with Merthyr Tydfil to Treharris (4/3/1916 to 19/4/1916), Caerphilly to Bargoed (August 1915 to 19/5/1917) and Caerphilly to Senghenydd (6/5/1916 to 19/5/1917), but all were abandoned. Nevertheless, it is interesting to note that Gower R.D.C., refused all of the company's applications, as it was considered that the area was sufficiently covered by other operators.

During the war years, there was petrol rationing, but nobody can recall the ungainly gas balloons strapped on top of the buses. During World War II, buses again had recourse to the use of gas, but the method of production was eminently more suitable and tidy.

The first fifteen AEC buses were purchased by the company in 1919, and formed an association with AEC which lasted 53 years.

THE ROARING TWENTIES

With the end of hostilities there was a period of retrenchment, but from 1920, and for the next ten years, the company established itself rapidly. Many new services were introduced and those already in operation were being extended. In addition, services of other operators together with their fleets of buses were being acquired wherever possible.

A successful bid to take over the gas-powered trams owned by Neath Council, was made in August 1920, replacing them with motor buses, and from July 1923 the company rented the old tram depot as their Neath garage. In May 1923, the Gower route from Swansea to Port-Eynon, was secured by the takeover of Fairwood Motors Ltd., at Swansea, and in July 1928, the business of Bishopston & Murton Bus Service, Bishopston was acquired with a service jointly operated by Swan Motors of Bishopston, running between Swansea and Bishopston. The business of Albert Thomas, Tirydail, Ammanford was absorbed December 1927 with a route from Ammanford to Llandeilo, and the rental of Thomas' garage at Tirydail for a short period.

This rear entrance AEC 'Y' type bus was new in 1923. Registered CY 6198 it carried a 26 seat timber framed body built by Brush.

From early in the 1920's, buses which were previously only allowed to operate from the periphery of the boundary of the Borough of Swansea, were allowed to run into the town. There was a stipulation that the fares to be charged within the town were to be in excess of those charged by the tramways. The rule was afterwards frozen, not to allow further operators entry into Swansea.

The company at that time was not only concerned with traffic in the Swansea area, but also in the neighbouring towns of Neath, Llanelli, and Pontardawe, and by the mid-twenties, depots had been established in each of these towns, with services operating to Carmarthen, Pontardulais, Ammanford, Ystradgynlais, Banwen, Maesteg and Abergwynfi, by June 1924. Pontardawe depot opened last of all in 1928, with an area of 728 square yards, housing 19 vehicles.

The rapid growth of the company was almost unbelievable, and the 1920's probably represented the most exciting and adventurous era in its history. It was a challenge to its staff at that time too, for it must not be forgotten that bus travel was in its infancy. The vehicles themselves were, by today's standards, very much of the hit-or-miss type, with no self-starter motors, and no windscreens. The general comfort for passengers and crews alike, was hardly the keynote, with solid rubber tyres, poor lighting, and harsh springing. Coupled with all this, roads were in a bad condition with pot-holes and ruts abounding.

All this, together with cut-throat competition from their competitors, was the issue of the company's staff in those early days. On many occasions, the privilege of carrying passengers was literally fought for. Timetables were something that appeared to only give a rough idea of starting times, after which, the devil took the hindmost in the fight for passengers. It was certainly the survival of the fittest, and how the company's staff thrived, can be gauged by the very large number of staff that were engaged in those hectic years, and were still loyally serving 50 years later.

One cannot leave this era without mentioning a major breakthrough in bus operation by the company. Within a few years after the 1914-1918 war, the Swansea Corporation embarked on a major house building scheme. The sites chosen were Townhill and Mayhill, Swansea, some 518 feet above sea level. To reach the summit, it was necessary to negotiate a road some 1.5 miles in length with gradients varying from 1 in 13, to 1 in 5.6, a formidable task for vehicles in the mid-1920's, having regard to passenger safety. After much experimenting and many tests, it was decided that what was good enough for Alpine climbing in Switzerland, must be good enough for Townhill, and consequently the company purchased a number of Swiss 'Saurer' 26 seater buses with a ratchet device to avoid the possibility of vehicles running backward on the hill. Drivers were specially trained for this type of bus, and in negotiating the hill itself. Even after overcoming all the 'hill' difficulties, passengers had to be persuaded that travel to Townhill via Mount Pleasant Hill and Penygraig Road was as safe as the houses they lived in, and to prove this point, many free rides were given at the inauguration of this service in April 1926. In 1929, the service was augmented to cater for people living in the Mayhill area.

Many other housing estates by private builders had also been completed in the western areas of the town, and to cater for the needs of the inhabitants, bus services were continually being extended. Neither were the areas outside the town ignored, nor was the constant vigilance to acquire the services of other operators relaxed. Even the operation of the Mumbles Railway was taken over by the South Wales Transport Company in 1927, and under powers already obtained, the electrification of the line was immediately undertaken.

The last steam train ran in March 1929, replaced by 106 seater electric railcars weighing 30 tonnes each. They could be operated in pairs, and on bank holidays, could carry up to 40,000 people.

Nevertheless, the financial position of the company during these depression years of the late 1920's, early 1930's was very poor with no dividends paid to the shareholders from 1928 to 1937.

The cut-throat competition mentioned earlier was now leading to what could almost be termed as 'piracy'. Uneconomical fares were being charged, and a great deal of wastage in buses and manpower came to alarming proportions amongst operators, including The South Wales Transport Co., merely to 'pinch' a few fares from their competitors. This was not exclusive to South Wales, and the tactic was rife throughout the country. Fortunately, some order eventually emerged from the chaos, with the passing of the 1930 Road Traffic Act, which also introduced the Traffic Commissioners. The whole country was divided into regions with Commissioners who were responsible for each region, working under a full time Chairman.

The Traffic Commissioners with the power vested in them, brought about stability of fares and an adherence to timetables. The granting of licenses to operate services which, hitherto, had been under the jurisdiction of local authorities, could now only be obtained through the new authority. Licenses to drive or conduct a public service vehicle were also their responsibility. The Road Traffic Act 1930, also assured drivers of sufficient rest periods and limited their hours of work. Before the advent of the Commissioners, there was the rather farcical position that a driver had to carry as many as three or four badges to show that he was entitled to drive in each particular town or area, within his scheduled journey.

These are badges which had to be worn by a driver to show that he was licenced to drive in the particular town or area shown on the badge. Assuming his scheduled journey took him through all four places, he would have to show the lot.

EXPANSION

In 1930, The South Wales Transport Company acquired control of the Swansea Improvements & Tramways Company, the town's tramway system. There had been a very close link between both companies ever since the inauguration of South Wales Transport in 1914, as the directors and management were common to both companies.

Venturing into a new sphere of business in 1933, the company purchased a pair of luxury touring coaches fitted with armchair seating and folding sunshine roofs. These coaches paved the way to a very popular holiday programme which was second to none.

Three more competitors were absorbed in 1935. They were J.M. Bacus of Burry Port with their share of Llanelli – Burry Port – Carmarthen in May 1935; Gwendraeth Transport Co., Ltd., of Pontyates with their share of Llanelli – Pontyates – Carmarthen in May 1935; and Willmore Motors of Neath with the Neath to Margam route in November 1935. Treharne Brothers of Ponthenry were acquired July 1936 with a service from Ponthenry to Llanelli via unclassified road to Cynheidre, and John Brothers of Grovesend with a service Neath – Morriston – Llanelli, and a local Gorseinon service, and also an express service to Porthcawl, in July 1936. Osborne Bus Services of Neath were absorbed in June 1937 with services Neath to Banwen, and Birchgrove to Briton Ferry. Last of all, in September 1938 the two services of Gorseinon & District (T. John) were taken over. They were Gorseinon to Penllergaer, and Llanrhidian to Llanelli, but mysteriously the 5 buses passed to the Red & White group just 3 months before they formed United Welsh Services as a subsidiary.

By 1935, however, the company came to the conclusion that the Swansea tramways were approaching the end of their usefulness, and therefore decided to ask Parliament for powers to abandon them. It was a rather complicated procedure, as certain tramway routes were leased from the Swansea Corporation, with whom agreement had to be reached. This was achieved, and resulted in the passing of The Swansea and District Transport Act, 1936, which empowered the company to operate services in the County Borough of Swansea for 21 years, during which time, it had to pay the Swansea Corporation a proportion of its profits or £5,000 per annum whichever was the greater. The Act also provided for the setting up of a Transport Advisory Committee, comprised of three representatives of The South Wales Transport Co., who met quarterly. That Committee has since relinquished all interest in the operation.

Most of the Tramway Company's staff were trained in bus operation, and to their credit and the credit of their tutors, there were few failures. Those who for one reason or another could not make the grade, were found other jobs within the company, and those who by reason of age or other factors could not be fitted in, were compensated by a lump sum based on years of service or by pension.

The changeover from trams to buses was effected in two operations; the first in 1936 took in the Morriston, Brynhyfryd and Cwmbwrla sections, and it was not until July 1937 that Sketty, Brynmill and Port Tennant sections were operated by buses. A total of 62 new AEC and 12 Leyland double decker buses were acquired to replace the 78 trams, and were legally owned by the Swansea Improvements & Tramways Company.

The tramway depot was considered inadequate to house the large number of additional motor vehicles, and accordingly freehold land was purchased at Ravenhill, Swansea, upon which a garage to house 140 vehicles was built. In addition, a new central workshops was erected on the site, where everything was overhauled 'in house'. The cost of erecting these buildings was £57,758, on 8,174 square yards of land purchased at £2,268. Additionally, the 'new' central workshops covered 2,472 square yards of land at Ravenhill.

11

The abandonment of the tramways system was not without its critics, who were mainly concerned about the ability of the bus to carry the number of passengers, who used the trams and the issue of the housewife with her shopping basket. This fear was quickly dispelled, for besides purchasing double decker buses of large capacity, the frequency of services, mobility and decreased journey times more than out-weighed any advantage the tram might have had in its carrying capacity.

It was unbeknown how wise the decision to abandon the tramway system was at that particular time, as within two years of the buses taking over, the country was at war again. The town of Swansea took a beating with the number of blitzes it received, one of which almost completely razed the town centre. Swansea suffered 44 air raids between June 1940 and February 1943, resulting in 387 deaths. It is indeed difficult to assess whether the trams could have continued operating in those dark days. By their mobility, buses could, and were diverted to other roads to complete their journey, which trams would not have been able to do. Even so, the buses had their casualties too, one was destroyed through enemy action and worse, one member of the company's staff was killed while shepherding his passengers to shelter.

Further land was acquired at Copperworks Road, Llanelli on 25th March 1938, to build a new depot of 2,515 square yards, capable of housing 41 vehicles inside and 12 outside. The cost of erecting this building was £13,995, on leasehold land from Neville Druce & Co., the Copper works, Llanelli.

THE POST WAR YEARS

At long last, World War II had come to an end. Staff who had been serving in other spheres during the war period, were now steadily returning to take up their places with the company, once again. Sorrowfully, there were a number of their colleagues who could not. For those who did return, the company did not present a very good picture. It could not, as the 'state of emergency' was still maintained, and under those powers, restrictions on fuel were not relaxed for some time afterwards. Nevertheless, there had been changes. For one, the role of the bus conductor, which had previously been assigned to men, in what had previously been deemed 'a man's world', was now shared with the opposite gender; conductresses, who had initially taken over the position during the war. There were changes in services too, for in the interest of National economy, it was agreed that some of the services in the Gower area, operated jointly with a neighbouring operator - The United Welsh Services Ltd., would be more easily operated by them alone. This pattern remained for some years after the cessation of hostilities, and eventually by an exchange of routes, the South Wales Transport Co., withdrew their services to Port Eynon, Rhossili, and Llanrhidian, as well as their Bishopston service, whilst the United Welsh Services, for their part, withdrew from operating services within the Swansea County Borough area.

By a gradual relaxation of the emergency powers, things in the transport industry were getting back to normal, Private Hire and Day Excursions were resumed and it was not long before the company was looking for fresh fields to conquer. In the early 1930's they had embarked upon Coach Tour Holidays to Scotland and North Wales which had proved very popular. Now that new coaches were becoming available again, thought was given to restarting this side of the company's business, only this time a far more ambitious scheme was devised, Continental Tour Holidays by coach. South Wales Transport were the first and only operator of Continental Tours in South Wales for many years, opening a booking office at Plymouth Street, Swansea on 29th September 1945.

The new tours were instantly successful, and it was obvious that the public who had been holiday starved for years were going to demand more and more. The company obliged, and the holiday programme grew bigger and bigger, going further afield to Switzerland, Austria, Germany, Spain, Portugal, Paris, Southern France, Italy, Belgium, Holland and Denmark. Naturally, staff had to be specially trained for this class of work. Drivers had to have knowledge of continental roads and adapt themselves to new conditions such as driving on the right hand side of the road, added to which they should have at least a sufficient knowledge of a foreign language to make themselves understood. Maybe in some respect, war had its uses, for a number of staff engaged on tours work had driven vehicles on continental roads during the war, and it's a poor man who can't find a way around any language difficulties. Nevertheless, at the outset couriers with knowledge of foreign languages were employed to accompany the tours. Later the company arranged tutorial language classes for drivers appointed to the continental driving staff. In this way experience was built up and passed on to other drivers making the grade. British tours were not neglected either, tours to Scotland, Ireland, Devon, Cornwall and other parts of Southern England all proved very popular.

As the years went by, the air was becoming a more and more popular mode of travel with certain sections of the public. The company quickly realised this and on the basic principle of 'if you can't beat them, join them', they came to an arrangement with air travel companies at Cardiff and Swansea to operate air tours. In fact holiday travel by all means of transport had by now become big business, and to cater for everyone's need and taste, the company set themselves up in the Travel Agency business. They were then appointed agents for all the major operators engaged in world travel, besides continuing to operate their own tours which were as popular as ever. To further their interest in this still extending travel field, the company opened a more commodious office at No. 6 Cradock Street, Swansea, near the town centre in August 1963, in preparation for the holiday business of 1964.

Incidentally, on the 29th September 1947, a shop was acquired at 70 Stepney Street, Llanelli for use as a traffic office, enquiry office and Holiday booking office.

As previously stated, the early 1950's saw the transport industry getting back to normal again, new vehicles were appearing on the roads to replace those which had done yeoman service during the war years and far beyond their normal span of life. It spoke well of the care with which these vehicles had been maintained by the company's engineering and maintenance staff that they were still roadworthy at the time of disposal.

Because of the general relaxation of the emergency conditions, the stage carriage side of the company's business had not been standing still, services which hitherto had been restricted had steadily increased in frequency to beyond pre-war standards. Private cars were at a premium then, and public transport in its heyday. Of major importance at this time was the purchase of the Llanelly & District Traction Company undertaking from the South Wales Electricity Board on the 22nd March 1952. The concern, previously owned by the Llanelly Electric Supply Co., (LLANESCO) Llanelli Power Station, had passed into S.W.E.B., ownership through nationalisation of the electricity industry in 1948. The State owned S.W.E.B., eventually decided they didn't want to operate a transport concern and sold it to the B.E.T., Group, initiating an act of de-nationalisation or privatisation.

The Llanelly & District Traction Co., operated trolleybuses and motor buses within the confines of Llanelli, and the new owners, South Wales Transport soon set about the task of scrapping the trolleybus system and substituted them with motor buses as quickly as it possibly could. Eleven new double decker motor buses were purchased to replace the trolleybuses, supplemented by older deckers within the fleet. As had happened with the Swansea tramways, as many as possible of the staff of the LL & D T Co., undertaking were trained as motor bus drivers. The last trolleybuses ran on Saturday 8th November 1952, being substituted by motor buses the following day.

Unfortunately at the end of the 1940's and the beginning of the 1950's the word 'cost' was rearing its head. For some time the company refrained from making an application to vary its fares, but increased taxation on fuel, increased cost of buying vehicles and steadily increasing wages made that action imperative in November 1950. It was the first application to increase its fares that the company had made since the appointment of the Traffic Commissioners in 1930. Regrettably, in the light of ever continuing inflation, more applications to increase fares had to be made thereafter on a regular basis. The problem was aggravated by the appearance of private motor cars on the roads in ever increasing numbers. Besides losing passengers to the private motor cars, the habits of the travelling public were also changing, for instead of the usual evening trips to cinemas, theatres etc., television was keeping them at home. All these factors were making heavy inroads into the number of passengers carried. This was the position even in 1957 when the Swansea Corporation elected to waive its right to operate the bus services in the County Borough after the expiry of the 21 years' lease which had been granted to the company under the terms of the Swansea and District Transport Act 1936. Their decision not to take up the option allowed the company to go about its business unfettered by fears of acquisition.

The South Wales Transport Company then embarked upon a big reconstruction scheme on its Brunswick and Ravenhill Garages. New equipment was installed to bring about an even greater efficiency and economy in operation and maintenance. At Pontardawe a completely new garage was built, and for its capacity was well equipped as any of its size in the country.

The 1960's era started on a very sad note when on the 5th January 1960, the famous Mumbles Railway undertaking ran its last tram, an occasion which was given worldwide coverage, such was its fame, and deservedly too, as it was the first passenger carrying railway to operate in the world. Before its closure the directors of South Wales Transport ordered a thorough investigation of the railway. Arising from this investigation it was found that to keep the trams going, a capital sum of at least £350,000 would be required. It was this coupled with rapidly increasing costs and a considerable fall in passengers carried which caused the directors to decide with great reluctance, to close down the undertaking. Ironically, the company had only bought the lease of the railway in September 1958! However, the railway was supplanted by the services of modern large capacity and well equipped double decker buses, and once again the public thought that the buses would not cope with the high capacity loads. They certainly did! Many of the railway staff were transferred to bus work as had happened when the Swansea tramways undertaking was abandoned in 1937. Those employees who by reason of age or other factors could not be absorbed were compensated.

Mention of large capacity buses in the previous paragraph serves as a reminder of the improvement in design technique, power, and the emphasis on comfort and safety of passengers, made by the vehicle manufacturers since the company came into existence. Throughout the years the company had kept abreast of the times with its vehicles and at all times in its history had been renowned for the smart appearance of its fleet.

It may be considered paradoxical to write of the company's further expansion at a period when throughout the road passenger transport industry the cries were; less passengers being carried, falling receipts, increasing costs and curtailment of services. In this respect, the company was no different from any other. On the 1st September 1962, they absorbed the business of J. James & Sons Ltd., Ammanford, an old established firm in the road passenger transport industry with roots dating back to 1888, operating services in the Amman Valley, Swansea Valley, and Gwendraeth Valley. The James business had been taken over by The British Electric Traction Co., Ltd., 12 years earlier, but had retained the James' identity. There had been a close association between James and South Wales Transport since the passing of the 'Road Traffic Act' in 1930. Both companies were joint operators on the Swansea Valley services and on sections of other services. This acquisition brought about a more economical operation and a link up of routes to give a better service to the travelling public and indeed some measures in this direction were taken immediately.

A detailed history of the James business, along with the companies they absorbed is currently still available from the publisher, Vernon Morgan at www.vernonmorgan.com

As the 1960's progressed, major issues had been brewing with regard to ownership of the company. The Labour Government of the period adopted a policy of extending public ownership of transport undertakings which inevitably led to the purchase of all the bus operating interests of B.E.T., in late 1967. Retaining the name The South Wales Transport Company Ltd., the company was then transferred to the Transport Holding Company (T.H.C.), which had been formed in 1962 to hold the shares of state owned companies, which already included those of the Tilling and Scottish Bus Groups. It was only a temporary arrangement as under the 1968 Transport Act, the National Bus Company (N.B.C.) was set up to take over the T.H.C., interests in England, Scotland and Wales, and in particular those formerly in the Tilling and B.E.T., groups. This came into operation on 1st January 1969.

The formation of N.B.C., caused major upheavals in South Wales with rationalisation of services and amalgamation of companies. Control of Thomas Bros. (Port Talbot) Ltd., and Neath & Cardiff Luxury Coaches Ltd., two smaller B.E.T. concerns were transferred to South Wales Transport in April 1969. The T.H.C., company; United Welsh Services Ltd., (previously Tilling owned) transferred to South Wales Transport in September 1970, all three being completely absorbed on 1st January 1971. The depots transferred to South Wales Transport with the companies were; Port Talbot (Thomas Bros.); Gorseinon, Neath Abbey, Clarence Terrace, Singleton Street and the Coach Station, Swansea (United Welsh).

Another upheaval for the company in 1971 was the loss of fifteen relatively new AEC Swift buses to N.B.C., subsidiary London Country Bus Services Ltd., as a result of legislation. The Swifts were replaced by fourteen Leyland single decker's around 15 years old as a stop gap until fifteen new Bristol RE buses could be diverted from the N.B.C., subsidiary, Western Welsh Omnibus Company's, delivery in 1971.

In addition, the services of Western Welsh, west of Porthcawl were taken over, together with vehicles and depots at Neath and Haverfordwest. The takeover at Neath was on 2nd January 1972, and that of Haverfordwest became effective on 26th March 1972. The W.W.O.C., depots at Newcastle Emlyn and New Quay were not taken over, they passed to N.B.C., subsidiary Crosville together with the services operated in the Cardiganshire area. W. W. O. Co's Carmarthen depot, together with Pontyberem and Laugharne outstations were closed down, these services passed to independent operators in Carmarthenshire.

During the same period 1971-2, there was a large influx of second-hand Bristol's from other N.B.C., subsidiaries. Many were Bristol MW6G coaches, which were converted into service buses with power operated entrance doors and 45 bus seats. However, these proved to be very unpopular with staff working town services, as they were fitted with constant mesh 'crash' gearboxes. This may well have been a contributing factor of the staff shortages of the period.

In August 1972, the N.B.C.'s poppy red livery with white band and grey wheels was adopted for service buses, with coaches adopting National White livery, and semi-coaches in poppy red and white.

Another change of company policy came about in 1973, this was the introduction of light weight chassis, Bedford's into the fleet, followed by 35 Ford R1014's a year later. The other intake of new vehicles during the 1970's and early 1980's were the integrally built Leyland National's which numbered 121 in total; 91 Bristol VR's, and some Leyland Leopard's. The introduction of the company's first minibuses came in 1977, when two second-hand Ford Transit's were acquired to operate a new 'Gower Pony' service between Gower and

Mumbles. Due to their success they were replaced by two new Bedford CF minibuses in 1980, but this wasn't the start of the minibus era!

1978 saw the opening of a long awaited new bus station in Swansea, built as part of the city centre redevelopment, close to the company's out dated coach station at Singleton Street. The new development called the 'Quadrant Centre' owned by the local authority was constructed with 25 bus departure bays and covered accommodation for bus and coach users, adjacent to a modern new shopping area. Incidentally, the whole bus station was rebuilt and modernised over an 18 month period 2009-10!

Mr D.J.R. Bending had become General Manager of the company from 1980, and combined this position with General Manager at National Welsh (previously Western Welsh) in 1984.

The return of a Conservative Government in 1979, and their new Transport Act of 1980 put renewed emphasis on competition, and at first this was largely concentrated on coach services. One brave local operator decided to compete against the National Express services operated by the company and joined a group of nation-wide operators calling themselves 'British Coachways'. The competitor, Morris Bros., of Swansea purchased ten new Volvo B58, Plaxton coaches to operate this network of coach routes, which inevitably fell by the wayside in 1984 and took Morris Bros., into receivership.

This occurred during the depression of the early 1980's, which also hit the mining and steel industries of South Wales along with the South Wales Transport Co., calling for many service cuts and a depot closure.

February 1982 was a noteworthy date within the company's history, for on 27th February 1982 the very last AEC Regent operated for the company after a 50 year association with the 'Regent' mark. GWN 867E (839), originally numbered (639), a 27 feet long example from the final batch of Regent's delivered in 1967 was the last to operate. However, it is pleasing to see that this bus has survived and now restored into pristine condition with the Swansea Bus Museum, and operates local tours on event days!

The last five AEC Regent's in service were replaced by five new specially built Bedford YMQS (shortened YMQ chassis) and fitted with Lex Maxata 37 seat bus bodies, which were built to meet a requirement, to negotiate a tight corner on service 14 near Pennard. Purchasing these Bedford's was a costly exercise for the company, as 3 years later they were surplus to requirement and passed to N.B.C., subsidiary Thames Valley. The local authority had carried out a road improvement, removing the notorious corner.

At this point in 1982, the fleet was changing rapidly, not only the last AEC's had gone but the last Neath & Cardiff and Thomas Bros., vehicles had also. On the other hand, the coaching side of the company had gained further opportunities when National Travel (South West) transferred their activities in Swansea to the company, with effect from April 1981. The 23 coaches acquired in the transfer gave a temporary reprieve to Brunswick Street depot's threatened closure. But instead, the former United Welsh depot at Clarence Terrace, Swansea, closed with the 25 vehicles it housed transferring to Brunswick Street Swansea, in April 1981.

Another interesting development at the coaching unit materialised in April 1982 when two MAN SR280 coaches were hired for a 13 month period to operate a new high speed service between Swansea and London (Victoria Coach Station) via the M4 Motorway in 3 hours 30 minutes. This was part of the N.B.C.'s new network of express services called 'Rapide', which was very successful. The company soon received fourteen new Leyland Tiger – Duple

Caribbean coaches to operate the network of 'Rapide' express services, followed by three new Plaxton Paramount 4000 bodied, Auwarter-Neoplan double decker coaches.

DEREGULATION

Then along came the 1985 Transport Act which laid down that all N.B.C., subsidiaries were to be privatised; selling off the individual companies. Another major issue of the Act was 'deregulation', meaning the opening up of services to competitors. This was opening up a new can of worms – basically going back to the way services operated before the 1930 Road Traffic Act was implemented. Deregulation finally took place in October 1986, introducing a new era of competition.

Nevertheless, the company fell in line with other N.B.C., subsidiaries at a time of ever decreasing passenger numbers, by running frequent services with minibuses and introducing services to previously unserviceable housing estates. Commencing in February 1986 with 19 seater Mercedes Benz L608D 'van derived' minibuses, the services were a success and paved the way to further minibus orders and minibus routes. New drivers were recruited to operate these services at a lower rate of pay. Longer serving drivers retained their higher rate of pay, operating 'conventional' buses. Introduction of the minibuses brought with it a new livery of two-tone green (lime green and leaf green) with red and yellow relief, a very pleasing alternative to all over red. This livery was eventually adopted for all vehicles after April 1987.

1986 also marked the departure of the last AEC's from the fleet. The last three AEC Reliance's, (180-2) were the end of an era, an association with AEC that had spanned 67 years. Another important feature of 1986 was the government's request that all N.B.C., companies be sold off separately to eliminate monopolies, and that no relationship with N.B.C., headquarters should be made in preparation for the selloff.

On the 30th January 1987, Creamline Services of Tonmawr suddenly ceased trading. Their services were absorbed by The South Wales Transport Co., the following day, 31st January.

At this point the company's General Manager, Mr D.J.R. Bending was appointed M.D. of The South Wales Transport Co., Ltd., and together with his management team considered the possibilities of a management buy-out. Under the leadership of David Bending and Alan Kreppel, The South Wales Transport Co., Ltd., was purchased from the N.B.C., on 8th May 1987, and was finalised in April 1988, with a fleet of 265 vehicles.

In the first year after privatisation, no less than three companies were absorbed. The first one in January 1988 was the business of A.E. & F.R. Brewer at Caerau, who were established in 1921. Not directly absorbed by S.W.T., it was acquired by the 'new' management team, at that time having the strange name of 'Novel Cobra Ltd'. This was a company formed to acquire S.W.T., from N.B.C., but shortly after privatisation in April 1988, the name Novel Cobra Ltd., was changed to United Welsh Holdings Ltd., resurrecting a company name that S.W.T., had abandoned in 1971. United Welsh Holdings however, became the holding company for S.W.T., Brewers and Llynfi Motor Services Ltd., of Maesteg, another established operator absorbed by the company in July 1988 with 17 vehicles. It must be mentioned here that after the Brewers take-over, an assortment of 34 vehicles entered S.W.T.'s fleet, eleven of which were A.E.C.'s, reviving the company's link with the mark. The Llynfi fleet was merged with the nearby Brewers fleet and the Llynfi name soon discarded.

In December 1988, the Swansea operations of Capitol Coaches, (owned by J. D. Cleverly of Cwmbran) were taken over together with five vehicles. This acquisition became the basis for a new coaching unit called United Welsh Coaches Ltd., and operated from the former S.W.T., Gorseinon depot, previously the United Welsh Services Ltd., depot. The United Welsh Coaches livery was basically white, with red, lime green and leaf green stripes, a different layout of the new S.W.T., livery. United Welsh Coaches was set up initially to challenge the numerous small operators in the area.

In early 1990 however, United Welsh Holdings Ltd., sold the three companies: South Wales Transport, Brewers, and United Welsh Coaches to Badgerline Holdings PLC., who also operated other former N.B.C. companies in the south-west of England and Essex. The three company names South Wales Transport, Brewers and United Welsh Coaches were retained along with the legal address and operator licence number PG 421.

Successful tendering for Dyfed County Council 'Bws Dyfed' network of tendered services in August 1990, expanded operations in that county substantially, requiring a depot in Carmarthen. The Carmarthen outstation, controlled by Llanelli depot was located at Cillefwr Industrial Estate, Johnstown, next door to J & P Bevan, the Mercedes Benz dealers who also carried out some of the company's maintenance. The services gained were Haverfordwest, Aberaeron, Llandeilo, Llandovery, Trelech and Pendine, challenging four smaller local operators.

In April 1995, it was announced that 'Badgerline Holdings PLC' had agreed terms with G.R.T. Bus Group PLC for a merger, creating a brand new group called First Bus PLC. G.R.T., formerly Grampian Regional Transport, was a bus group based in Aberdeen with Moir Lockhead as its chairman.

The merger went ahead as planned on 16th June 1995 following clearance by the Monopolies & Mergers Commission and the English and Scottish Courts. First Bus PLC., a Scottish registered company was the second largest bus group in the U.K., with a fleet of 5,600 vehicles. Moir Lockhead of G.R.T., became chief executive and Trevor Smallwood of Badgerline became executive chairman of a company with 20 subsidiaries. All vehicles began to receive 'First Bus' logo stickers in their rear windows from mid-June, replacing the familiar 'Badger' logo, but the S.W.T., Brewers and United Welsh Coaches trading names continued to be used, along with the operators licences. The United Welsh Coaches depot at Gorseinon was changed to outstation status for Port Talbot depot in March 1995, and was vacated in June 1996.

Expansion of the company continued, with all the stage carriage services operated by 'D' Coaches of Morriston and their associates; Rees & Williams / West Wales Motors, of Tycroes, and Glantawe Coaches, Morriston being absorbed in January 1996. The 'D' Coaches premises at Pontardulais Road, Tycroes (formerly owned by Rees & Williams Ltd.) was also acquired along with 9 vehicles and road service licences. 'D' Coaches had acquired the Rees & Williams business in August 1987 with a proviso that the Rees & Williams name continued. This proviso passed over into S.W.T., ownership as a fleet name only.

Nine months later in October 1996, the stage carriage services of Porthcawl Omnibus Company Ltd., were absorbed, and in March 1997, all the services operated by Davies Bros. (Pencader) Ltd., from their Trimsaran depot were acquired without any vehicles or premises. This was the first part of Davies Bros., to be absorbed, the final part was purchased in June 1999 when Davies Bros., went into receivership. Their remaining services, contracts, new depot at Glangwili, Carmarthen, and 39 vehicles were all acquired by 'First Cymru Buses Ltd.,' the successor to First Bus PLC.

First Cymru Buses Ltd., was formed in April 1998 to re-organise the operations of First Bus PLC., and to discard the separate trading names, i.e: South Wales Transport, Brewers and United Welsh Coaches, together with those operator licences. The fleet name 'First Cymru' had been applied to all vehicles by May 1998, yet the legal lettering and operator licences remained as South Wales Transport. The legal lettering was finally changed to 'First Cymru Buses Ltd'., on 28th March 1999, and the new operator licence; PG 421 was issued in the name of First Cymru Buses Ltd., on 31st May 1999.

This then would be the correct date of The South Wales Transport Company's demise. It is interesting to note that the 'O' licence number, PG 421 (later renumbered PG 0000421) was the same number that had been carried by South Wales Transport since 1931!

This is the fascinating story of The South Wales Transport Company's 100th anniversary. A story briefly and simply told, but between its pages lies a record of public service difficult to surpass. Between its pages also are thousands and thousands of unwritten stories of men, women and families who have worked, lived and died in its service. It's a tribute to them all!

It must be pointed out that the current operator trading as 'South Wales Transport' in 2014 has no connection with the original company bearing that name.

This Milnes-Daimler 30hp was one of a pair acquired by the company with the business of F.L Lewis, Pontardawe in 1914.

One of the earliest vehicles purchased by South Wales Transport in 1914 was CY1512 a 32 seater Belsize. Belsize Motors Ltd of Clayton, Manchester did not manufacture large numbers of passenger chassis.

CY1526, a Leyland 40hp with British Electrical Manufacturing Co., B32R body, seen here at Llanelli Town Hall was one of the earliest vehicles to operate Swansea to Llanelli.

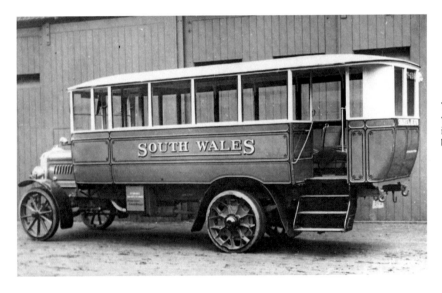

The first doubled decker's in the fleet were AEC 403 'S' types, which were new in 1922. They were also the first forward control buses delivered to the company, and were timber bodied by Fry, seating 54 passengers.

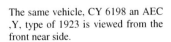

This rear entrance AEC 'Y' type bus was new in 1923. Registered CY 6198 it carried a 26 seat timber framed body built by Brush Coachworks.

The same vehicle, CY 6198 an AEC ,Y, type of 1923 is viewed from the front near side.

A selection of AEC YC's parked up at Brunswick Street depot in the 1920's.

This pair of AEC 503 charabancs, CY 6537/8 were bodied by Strachan & Brown as 32 seaters. They were very early touring coaches!

Photographed here before delivery in 1924 is another AEC 503, CY 6531 which was bodied by Ransomes of Ipswich as a 54 seater. It had the luxury of electric lighting.

CY 7084, another AEC 503 was one of the first South Wales Transport buses, to be fitted with pneumatic tyres. New in 1925 it was fitted with a B34R body built by Brush, and was sold in 1928.

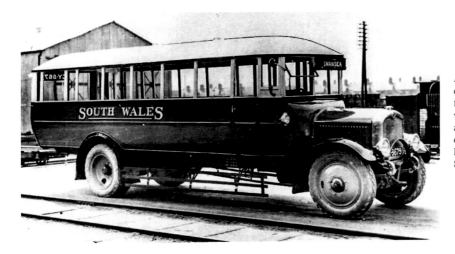

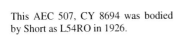

An initial batch of six Saurer single decker's were specially purchased for the Townhill route in 1926. They were manufactured in Switzerland and built specifically for hilly districts and bodied by Brush as B26R. This one was registered CY 8679.

This AEC 507, CY 8694 was bodied by Short as L54RO in 1926.

This AEC 507, CY 8682 of 1926 was the last open top, solid tyred bus acquired, and had 'herringbone' type seating, which was an early form of low-bridge type body, seating 54 passengers.

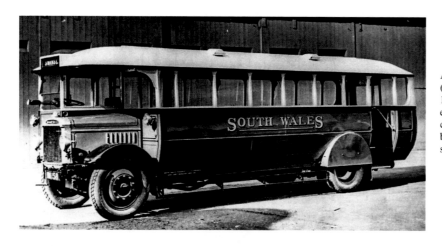

A batch of twelve ADC 416 (Associated Daimler Co) arrived in 1927, fitted with 6 cylinder Daimler engines in their AEC built 416 type chassis. Brush built their 26 seat bodies, this one was sold to a showman in 1932.

This Dennis ES of 1929, WN 1857 was fitted with a second hand Brush body from new. The body was off an early AEC YC chassis, and was rebuilt by SWT to seat 32.

One of the earliest buses to carry fleet numbers was this Dennis EV (206) WN 2579 of 1929. It had bodywork built by SWT themselves, to B32R layout.

This photograph is self-explanatory – the old Mumbles steam hauled train and the new 106 seat, electric tramcars of 1929. South Wales Transport took over the lease of the railway in 1927 and replaced the steam trains with the electric trams in 1929.

WN 4760 (260) was one of 50 AEC Regent double decker's with petrol engines acquired in 1932. Petrol engines were still standard fitment at this time, but were the last batch of petrol engined Regent's acquired. Their low-bridge bodies built by Brush seated 51.

This Tilling Stevens Motors demonstrator came to South Wales Transport in 1932 in full SWT livery. After a period of demonstration at SWT as fleet number 1, it was returned to TSM and afterwards sold to competitors Swan Motors of Bishopston. Registered KJ 2915, it was a TSM E60A6 fitted with Beadle L56R body.

Turning to a new sphere of operation, the company's first pair of touring coaches arrived in 1933. This AEC Ranger, WN 5400 (300) had Harrington 20 seat coachwork, fitted with armchair seating and folding roof. They were used on 4 to 9 day tours which were called 'Holiday Cruises'.

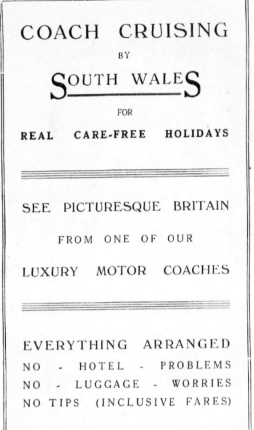

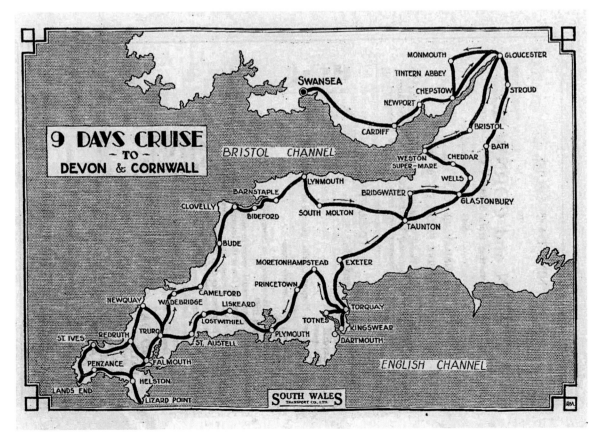

An extract from the Holiday Brochure of 1936. This particular tour to Devon & Cornwall was priced at £15-0-0 all inclusive.

South Wales Transport acquired this Leyland Lion, TH 1066 with the business of J.M.Bacus & Co., Burry Port in 1936. New in 1930, it carried a Leyland B32R body and received fleet number 369 during its short stay with the company.

This Beadle C32R bodied Leyland TS7c Tiger, BNY671 passed in to the SWT fleet in July 1936 with the business of John Brothers of Grovesend when it was just a month old.

WN 5815 (315) was one of a batch of five Townhill buses purchased in 1933. They were AEC Renown six-wheelers, fitted with 8.8 litre oil engines (the company's first diesel engine buses). Brush built their 40 seat rear entrance bodies.

The company acquired control of the Swansea tramway system in 1930, and eventually abandoned it in favour of 74 new double decker buses. Pictured here is car number 18 heading for St. Helens, Swansea, having just crossed the river Tawe on 1st April 1937. The building visible in the background was once a familiar landmark, the Weavers flour mills near Swansea Docks.

Swansea tramcar number 22 is captured here on route 5 to Swansea Docks in 1937.

This 'special' demonstrator AEC Renown six wheeler, MV 3711 (316) was taken into stock in October 1932. Built specially for the Townhill route with its steep gradients in mind, it was fitted with a sprag brake similar to that on the Saurer buses. It had a petrol engine, coupled to a pre-selective gearbox (which was optional), and a lightweight Park Royal body seating 38. It was scrapped in 1945.

Another demonstrator taken into stock in 1933 was this AEC Regal 0662 with 8.8 litre diesel engine and pre-selective gearbox, and again a sprag brake, for use on the Townhill route. Registered by AEC as AMD 48 it carried fleet number (317) and fitted with a Park Royal B32F body. This and Renown (316) were the first front entrance vehicles in the fleet.

Up until the outbreak of World War 2, Dennis chassis were not uncommon in the SWT fleet. In March 1934, another 12 new Dennis Lancet's with 4 cylinder petrol engines arrived, and were apparently quite economical! This one, WN 6218 (318) is pictured here when new, fitted with a Weymann B32R body. It was requisitioned by the War Department in September 1940 and not returned.

Other vehicles delivered in 1934 were eight AEC Renown's with 8.8 litre oil engines and pre-selective gearboxes, bodied by Weymann to L34/30R low-bridge layout. Pictured here when new is WN 6236 (336) one of the batch which worked the busy Swansea to Llanelli route jointly with Bassett's of Gorseinon, who also ran Renown's on the route

The only Daimler's acquired new by the company were five COG5's purchased in March 1935 for the Townhill route, after trials with a demonstrator. Seen here is WN 7740 (340) one of the five, fitted with Gardner 5LW engines, five speed gearboxes, low ratio axles and Weymann B35F bodies.

The first new Leyland's purchased since 1914 were six TS7 Tiger's with Weymann C28F touring coach bodies delivered in 1935. In 1948 the remaining four were rebuilt to B32R layout for stage carriage work as can be seen from this view of WN 7756 (706) at Llanelli Town Hall bus terminus c1954.

WN 7757 (705) is another Leyland TS7 Tiger rebuilt from a touring coach in 1948. With their 8.8 litre diesel engines, they were excellent performers on the Welsh hills. It is seen here at Broadway, Llanelli.

The AEC Q type was not a popular
choice of vehicle with the company.
Only five new and three second hand
were acquired despite their high
seating capacities of 39. These again
were purchased for the Townhill
route but suffered from cooling
problems. WN 8261 (361) seen here
before delivery in 1935 has a B39F
layout body built by Brush.

After delivery of the Leyland
Tiger's in 1935, a further order for
Leyland's arrived in 1936, in the
form of six 'Titans'. They were
WN 8984-9 (384-9) Leyland TD4's
with Weymann L29/26R metal
framed bodies. The first one
WN8984 (384) is seen here before
delivery to South Wales Transport
in 1936.

Eight AEC Regal ll's arrived in 1936,
fitted with 6.6 litre diesel engines. The
short bonnet allowed space for 39
seats in the body built by Brush, and
were again fitted with pre-selective
gearboxes. In 1945/6 they were retro-
fitted with 7.7 litre engines. Pictured
here at Castle Street, Swansea, is WN
9596, originally fleet number 396,
renumbered 23 in 1939.

A fleet of 62 AEC Regent double decker's were purchased for the Swansea tram replacement of 1936/7. ACY 8 (No.8) pictured here was one of the first batch registered ACY 1-50. They were all fitted with 7.7 litre engines, 'crash' gearboxes and Weymann steel framed bodies seating 56 to high-bridge layout. They were all legally owned by Swansea Improvements & Tramways Co., as stated on the vehicle's legal lettering. They were also the first high-bridge type decker's in the fleet.

ACY 9 pictured here started its working life as one of the tram replacement AEC Regent double decker buses in 1937, but received severe accident damage in a low bridge collision in 1952, resulting in its conversion to a tree-lopper come towing vehicle and driver trainer. It was also used to train the former trolleybus drivers at Llanelli in 1952.

By the time this photograph was taken at Oystermouth Road, Swansea, in 1954, this tram replacement AEC Regent, ACY 40 had been renumbered from 40 to 241, and repainted without the upper cream band and no louvers between decks, suggesting it had been re-panelled.

High-bridge bodied AEC Regent, ACY 49 (250) is captured here at Heol Pen-bre, Kidwelly, demonstrating the clearance beneath a railway bridge on the main A484 road to Llanelli. Because of the bridge's arched construction, double decker's had to negotiate it by traveling in the centre of the road, as demonstrated. Unfortunately, more than one double decker came to grief here!

The second batch of tram replacement buses consisted of twelve more AEC Regent Weymann double decker's built to the same design as the earlier examples. AWN554 (54) later renumbered 255, is seen here in a publicity photograph when new in July 1937, some of these saw 21 years' service with the company.

The Dennis Lancet ll with Dennis 04, four cylinder oil engine was the company's choice of single decker in 1937. The first batch comprised of twelve chassis with 39 seat bus bodies by English Electric. AWN 569 (69) is seen here in September 1948 after being re-numbered 857 in 1939. They were all scrapped in 1949.

The first twelve of the thirty-five Leyland Titan TD5 decker's placed in service in 1938 were legally owned by the Swansea Improvements & Tramways Company, as tram replacement buses. BCY 575 (75) was one legally owned by S.I.T.C., and was re-numbered 507 in 1939 in a fleet renumbering programme. It is seen here at Rhossili, in Gower, working a route that was eventually exchanged with competitors, United Welsh Services, for Swansea local services in the early 1950's.

Another TD5 from the same batch of tram replacement buses is BCY 582 (82), pictured here when new, showing the different style of fleet-name used on the tram replacement vehicles.

The penultimate batch of Dennis Lancet II's in 1938 were fitted with 4 cylinder oil engines and five speed gearboxes, with Dennis 32 seat coach bodies. Painted in coach livery, cream and black when new, they were renovated and repainted dark red in 1947/8 as seen here on BWN 320 (originally 120) re-numbered 868 in 1939.

Double decker deliveries of 1938/9 were entirely Leyland Titan's with Weymann low-bridge L27/26R bodies. BWN427 (544) a TD5 is captured here in Castle Street, Swansea, c1952, with CCY 975 (580) another Titan TD7 close behind.

Further AEC Renown's arrived in 1939, all fitted with Brush B39F bodies and 8.8 litre diesel engines for the Townhill service. Drive was to both rear axles. CCY 955 (155) seen here when new was re-numbered 40 in 1939 and remained in service until 1954.

CCY 958 (158) was numerically the first Dennis Lancet 2, from the last batch ordered in 1939. Re-numbered 885 soon after delivery, it is seen here in post-war years at Oystermouth Station (Mumbles Railway) bound for Langland Bay. It carried a Weymann B39F body to BET federation design, and was withdrawn in 1949, just 10 years old!

The final batch of Leyland double decker's delivered to the company in 1939 were twenty five Leyland Titan TD7's with Weymann low-bridge bodies identical to the 1938 TD5 deliveries. CCY 979 (179) later re-numbered 588 is seen here before delivery, with the fleet-name style reverting back to pre-1937 deliveries.

All of the AEC Renown's purchased by the company were ordered initially for the Townhill route, and fitted with 8.8 litre engines. In later days, several were re-engined with smaller 7.7 litre units and used on other routes, as can be seen in this view of Brush bodied CWN 400 (48) previously numbered 200, working to Jersey Marine. It was the last Renown purchased, joining a fleet of 322 vehicles with the company.

Llanelli (Robertson St.) depot is the backdrop for this view of EWN 338 (305) a 1948 AEC Regent ll with Weymann H30/26R bodywork. It's captured here at the former Llanelli trolleybus depot about to leave on former trolleybus route L1 in July 1959. The tram lines in the foreground date from the horse-drawn tram era, and still remain there in 2014. The advertising board against the wall advertises the company's day tours to Aberavon Beach, Port Eynon and New Quay, Cardiganshire.

Captured here at Rutland Street, Swansea, close to the Mumbles Railway tram depot is EWN 342 a 1948 AEC Regent ll carrying its original fleet number 288. In 1958 it was re-numbered 1100 in a scheme to re-number all low-bridge double decker's in a separate series. Its low-bridge body was built by Weymann to L27/26R layout, and was one of only twenty ever built on AEC Regent ll chassis.

The 1949 order for new buses included another ten Townhill single decker's, FCY 342-351 (61-70). They were AEC Regal lll's with large 9.6 litre engines, pre-select gearboxes and air brakes, with Willowbrook B34F bodies. Pictured here is one of the batch, FCY 344 (63) working service 12A to Mayhill (Townhill), at Grove Place, Swansea, about to ascend Mount Pleasant Hill.

The first touring coaches purchased after World War 2 ended, arrived in 1949. They were FWN 82-4 (1001-3) AEC Regal lll's with Windover C30F bodies, painted in a new coach livery of all over Ivory with red relief and Gothic-style lettering as displayed here by FWN84 (1003). Air conditioning was an added luxury.

Low bridges prevented the use of normal height buses on many of the company's double decker routes, notably at Port-Tennant and Neath. AEC Regent lll Weymann, FWN 350 (1119) originally F/N 312 was one of nineteen low-bridge type decker's based at Neath depot, and is seen here at Castle Street, Swansea, working to Porthcawl via Neath, a route requiring the use of low-bridge type decker's only.

Looking in pristine condition is FWN 357 (319) a 1949 AEC Regent lll with 7ft.6inch wide Weymann 'high-bridge' body, working service No. 2 to Llanelli, (then spelt Llanelly). This was one of the company's earliest routes dating from 1914. 319 is captured here negotiating Kingsway roundabout in Swansea, a landmark removed in 2008 to accommodate the new 'bendy buses' of First Cymru.

FWN 506 (75) was another 'Townhill' bus built in 1949. It was another 9.6 litre engined AEC Regal lll with Willowbrook B34F bodywork, identical to the earlier batch Nos. 61-70. It is seen here at Belle Vue Way, Swansea, before the redevelopment of the area in the 1950's.

Longwell Green Coachworks at Bristol bodied only five vehicles for South Wales Transport. Seen here at Swansea High Street Railway Station on service No.1 from the Swansea Valley, is one of these rare saloons, FWN633 (104) an AEC Regal lll with 7.7 litre engine, manual gearbox and Longwell Green B34F body, built almost identical to the Willowbrook examples delivered earlier.

The 7.7 litre, 'crash gearbox' 6821A version of the AEC Regal lll looked outwardly the same as the 9.6 litre model. Here is one of the 39 smaller engined Regal lll's, FWN 808 (114) at Quay Parade, Swansea, in 1960; it's Willowbrook body looking rather tired.

Oystermouth bus/tram station in 1951 illustrates the typical AEC Regal lll Willowbrook combination, of which the company had 52. FWN 803 (109) is seen here working a local service to Newton.

In 1950 the last nine AEC Regal lll 6821A Willowbrook saloon's arrived, and were identical to the 1949 batch of 7.7 litre engined, manual transmission models. This one, GCY 306 (136) is seen here at Oystermouth Station working a Mumbles tram replacement service in 1959.

A large order of seventeen AEC Regal touring coaches arrived in 1950. GCY 442 (1015) pictured here was one of the first fourteen, AEC Regal lll Willowbrook bodied half-cab models, fitted with 9.6 litre engines and crash gearboxes. Unfortunately, half-cab coaches were about to become obsolete, and were replaced by modern looking fully fronted coaches after a few years.

The last three AEC Regal coaches from the 1950 order had the same chassis as above, but their Windover coachwork differed, being 8 feet wide, with full width cab's, modified front mudguards and more luxurious seating for Continental touring. They were the first 8 feet wide vehicles in the fleet. GCY 447 (1020) seen here when new was numerically the last one delivered. The trio, GCY 445-7 (1018-20) seated 28 in adjustable reclining seats, but were re-seated to 30 in 1958.

Pictured here at Ravenhill depot when new in 1950 is the penultimate Willowbrook B34F bodied AEC Regal lll, GCY 472 (138) fitted with 7.7 litre engine and crash (manual) gearbox.

The 1950 delivery of double decker's were again AEC Regent lll chassis with Weymann bodywork. The batch of twenty-three were all of low-bridge L27/26R construction, and registered as GCY521- 543 (338-360). Captured here outside Neath depot circa 1960 is last of the batch; GCY 543 which had been re-numbered 1143 in 1958, (in a series for low-bridge decker's) along with the others.

By contrast, in 1951 the entire batch of again twenty-three buses delivered, were all high-bridge type. They were GWN 73-95 (361-383) AEC Regent lll's, with Weymann H30/26R bodies. 361-9 were 7ft.6inches wide, whilst 370-383 were 8ft. wide; by then a permissible width for 2 axle double decker's. Pictured here at Llanelli Town Hall Square is GWN 82 (370), numerically the first 8ft. wide AEC Regent in the fleet.

44

On 27th March 1952, the company absorbed The Llanelly & District Traction Co., at Llanelli. The undertaking latterly owned by The South Wales Electricity Board ran trolleybuses and motor buses in the Borough. South Wales Transport ran the trolleybuses only until 9th November 1952, when they were all replaced with motor buses and the system scrapped. The Leyland TB2 trolleybus pictured here at Pwll terminus in June 1952 was operating for South Wales Transport in full Llanelly & District livery, as were the other trolleybuses. (C. Carter)

Two more of the Llanelly & District Traction Co's., Leyland TB2 trolleybuses, with Leyland H30/26R bodies are seen here at Llanelli Railway Station terminus running for SWT in 1952.

CBX 913 (47) a Karrier W trolleybus with utility Park Royal H30/26R body was one of the newest taken over. It was new in 1946, and is captured here at Llanelli Station in 1952 running for SWT, on route 2 to Felinfoel. It was sold to Bradford Corporation after withdrawal, where it was re-bodied and operated until December 1970, when that system closed down also.

The motor buses acquired from Llanelly & District in 1952 were very quickly repainted into SWT livery, but retained their L. & D. T. C., fleet numbers. TH 7763 (29) an AEC Regal 0662 of 1936, with Beadle B35F body is seen here at Llanelli Town Hall bus station on route to Furnace, 1 mile out of town, in 1955.

Another AEC Regal 0662 taken over from Llanelly & District was ABX 902 (24) a 1938 model with Weymann B35F body. This was rebuilt to B28F with standing room for 23 passengers, and is seen here at Murray Street, Llanelli, outside the General Accident Insurance Company's office.

All of the motor buses acquired from Llanelly & District were built to a low overall height enabling them to negotiate the low bridges in the New Dock area of Llanelli. It can be seen from this view of CTH 930 (20) how low the roof line really was on its Strachan B35F body. Its AEC Regal 0662 chassis dating from 1946 was fitted with a 7.7 litre engine. The bus entered service in January 1947.

This ex. Llanelly & District AEC Regal lll, received its SWT livery long before the trolleybus system closed. It's pictured here at the junction of Robinson Street and Station Road in June 1952, on a local service to Tyisaf. Its special low height bodywork was built by Bruce Coachworks, Cardiff, in 1950. FTH 836 had fleet number 17, and was one of six of the type acquired – FTH 836-841. The roof of the Llanelli depot is just visible on the extreme right hand side, in Robinson Street.

There were six AEC Regal lll's acquired from Llanelly & District; FTH 836-841 (17, 18, 23, 30-32) all fitted with Bruce B35F bodies, specially built to negotiate the bridges at New Dock. This one, FTH 837 (18) is seen at Trinity Road negotiating a 9ft.3inch bridge with not much clearance

The Llanelly trolleybus system was abandoned on 8th November, 1952, and superseded by motor bus operation the following day with higher fares. Eleven new AEC Regent lll decker's, with Weymann H30/26R bodywork, ordered by Llanelly & District were delivered direct to SWT for the trolleybus replacement programme. Nine of the batch are pictured here before delivery to Llanelli in 1952. The eleven were registered HWN 837-847 (414-424).

47

One of the trolleybus replacement buses; HWN846 (423) an AEC Regent lll with Weymann H30/26R bodywork is seen here working service L2, a former trolleybus route across town, Felinfoel to Llanelli Railway Station. The location: Broadway, Llanelli, disappeared under a re-development scheme, in 1962.

Another Llanelly trolleybus replacement vehicle, AEC Regent lll, HWN840 (417) is seen here at Llanelli Town Hall Square, working another cross-town service Llanelli Railway Station to Cefn Caeau estate, 2 miles east of town. These buses spent almost their entire working life on Llanelli local services.

This particular trolleybus replacement vehicle, HWN 838 (415) is seen leaving the former trolleybus depot at Robinson Street, Llanelli, in 1960. The depot office; formerly a stable in the days of Llanelli's horse drawn trams, is just visible on the left. Additionally, the tram lines on the depot floor are still in place today, 2014, in the depot owned by First Cymru Buses.

An additional fifteen low-bridge AEC Regent's arrived in 1952, again bodied by Weymann to L27/26R layout. They were of the 9613A type chassis, registered HCY 827-841 (384-398), renumbered into the low-bridge series in 1958 as 1144-58. HCY 838, by now renumbered 1155 is seen at Princess Way, Swansea, on route 42 to Margam – a route requiring the low-bridge type decker's.

The first under-floor engined vehicles for the company arrived after the Commercial Motor Show of 1952, but didn't enter service until 1953. They were a pair of AEC Regal IV, 9621E models with 9.6 litre horizontal engines and pre-select gearboxes. Registered HWN 722/3 (1021/2) they were fitted with very unusual Windover 35 seat coachwork, with rear entrances.

The last deliveries of AEC's with the traditional exposed radiator were the 1953 batch of Regent lll, 9613S models, with Weymann low-bridge L27/26R bodies of semi-lightweight construction. The batch of fifteen were registered HWN 895-909 (399-413) and were later renumbered 1159-73 in the low-bridge series as seen on HWN 907 (1171) parked here at St. Mary's Square, Swansea, circa 1963.

The 1954 order for double decker's consisted of another fifteen low-bridge type AEC's. They were AEC Regent lll, 9613S chassis, with Weymann 'Orion' lightweight bodies, seating 56, and had the so-called 'New Look' enclosed radiator grilles offered by AEC as an option at the time. They were registered JWN 901-15 (425-439) renumbered 1174-88 in 1958. Eight of them were fitted with platform doors from new, as seen by JWN 908 (1181) here at Kingsway, Swansea, in 1962. This particular bus is now awaiting restoration at the Swansea Bus Museum.

A second pair of Windover C35R bodied AEC Regal IV touring coaches arrived in 1954. They were identical looking coaches, but this pair JWN 916/7 (1023/4) had modified chassis, of the type 9822E. These coaches were used on extended tours when new, but JWN 916 pictured here is seen at Tenby coach park.

AEC's introduced a new lighter double decker chassis at the 1954 Commercial Motor Show, known as the Regent V model. SWT received the first 20 production examples of model MD3RV Regent V's in 1955, bodied by Weymann with 'Orion' medium-weight bodies. They were MCY 400-19 (440-59). The first ten were high-bridge, and the last ten low-bridge, and some had platform doors. Numbers 450-59 were renumbered 1189-98 in 1958. MCY 407 (447) seen here is now in preservation at the Swansea Bus Museum.

One of the low-bridge Weymann 'Orion' double decker's received in 1955 is pictured here at Kingsway, Swansea, in 1956/7 carrying its original fleet number 455. Registered MCY415 it was renumbered 1194 in 1958. The engines fitted were the AV470 units of 7.7 litres.

MCY 420 was number 801 when new but was renumbered 1801 in 1961. It had the horizontal AH470 equivalent of the AV470 (vertical) engine, used in the 1955-57 batches of double decker's. The fleet of eight new buses for the Townhill route in 1955, MCY 420-7 were examples of the AEC Reliance model introduced in 1953. The body design was basically the standard Park Royal 44 seat design as introduced for this chassis, but the SWT chassis were noteworthy in being MU2RA models with the 'Monocontrol' epicyclic gearbox, eliminating the clutch pedal.

The company acquired eight new touring coaches for the 1956 season in the form of AEC Reliance's with Weymann Fanfare C37F coachwork. The Fanfare coach body design was very successful, being favoured by several BET companies. They were fitted with 5 speed synchromesh gearboxes. Seen here is MWN 571 (1025) complete with its roof mounted air horns. It was the first of the 1956 delivery; MWN571-3 and NCY622-6 (1025-32).

The delivery of Weymann Fanfare coaches in 1956 arrived in two batches, ousting some of the AEC Regal lll coaches. Numerically the last one of the second batch was NCY626 (1032) seen here, which is now preserved at the Swansea Bus Museum. A further five of this model were purchased in 1958; PWN 64-8 (1033-7).

More high-bridge type AEC Regent V's appeared in 1956, all with light-weight Weymann 'Orion' H32/28R bodies. Their chassis were type MD3RV with AV470, 7.7 litre engines, and registered NCY 451-71 (460-80). NCY 463 (472) is seen here at Llanelli Town Hall bus station in 1963.

AEC Regent V, NCY 455 (464) is seen here in the yard of Llanelli depot in 1964. The office and yard in the foreground, previously owned by The South Wales Electricity Board had only been acquired in 1963, giving the company extra space to their adjacent yard and buildings at Robinson Street depot, which had been purchased from S.W.E.B., with the Llanelli trolleybus undertaking in 1952. Acquiring this extra land led to the closure of the company's Copperworks Road depot in Llanelli, in 1964.

Twenty more AEC Regent V, type MD3RV were ordered for 1957 delivery, but this order was split between two body-builders. OCY 664-73 (481-90) were bodied by Weymann to H32/28R layout; OCY 674-83 (491-500) were bodied by Willowbrook to H32/28R layout. These were the last AEC Regent's purchased new with rear entrances. Pictured here is Weymann bodied OCY 666 (483) at Oystermouth Station, (Mumbles Railway).

The style of bodywork carried on the Willowbrook bodied Regent's was completely different, as can be seen from this photograph of OCY 675 (492). The Willowbrook body was more rounded and had a four bay construction compared to Weymann's five bay. The rounded off front mudguards were a modification carried out by SWT on all Regent V's after 1960.

The company entered a new era of double decker buses in 1958 with delivery of 26 front entrance AEC Regent V's, type LD3RA. Fitted with 9.6 litre engines, they were the first decker's with air brakes, and built to the new permitted length for two axle buses of 30 feet. They were all bodied by Weymann to H39/32F layout, as shown in this view of RCY 352 (510). The batch were registered RCY 343-68 (501-26) and renumbered 701-26 in 1970. Six of them 504/8/11/6/9/26 were delivered and operated in an 'unpainted' aluminium finish as an experiment for several years. After withdrawal in 1972, four were sold to a local competitor, Eynon's of Trimsaran. This was a very unusual type of practice.

Developed in conjunction with B.E.T. companies that needed low height double decker's was the AEC Bridgemaster. Built in 1958 with independent front suspension and of integral construction, it was assembled by Park Royal Coachworks. SWT were one of the first customers for this new type of bus which seated 72 people. These new style low-bridge buses, RCY 369-72 (1199-1202) arrived in 1959 and were a tremendous improvement in design compared to the sunken side-gangway decker's. Last of the batch, RCY 372 (1202) is seen here operating one of the low bridge routes to Port Tennant, Swansea.

SWN 980 (809) seen here at Maesteg when new, was one of a batch of AEC Reliance 2MU3RV's ordered in 1959. All fitted with Park Royal B45F bodies; SWN 980-4 (809-13) were delivered in 1959, the remaining five from the same order SWN 985-9 (814-8) with 2MU2RA type chassis (epicyclic gearbox) for the Townhill route arrived in 1960. These had identical Park Royal B45F bodies.

Continuing with the same block of vehicle registration numbers in 1959, SWN 990-6 (527-33) were further AEC Regent V type 2D3RA's with Weymann H39/32F bodies, of which 527/9/33 were delivered in an 'unpainted' aluminium finish as an experiment. Last of the batch, SWN 996 (533) is seen here at Swansea's Oxford Street, operating in its unpainted form.

Four new coaches were delivered in 1959. Built on AEC Reliance 2MU3RV chassis with Weymann bus framed body shells, they were built to coach standards. Registered as SWN 997/8; TCY 3/4, (1038-41) they were classified as dual purpose vehicles and had 41 coach seats. Relegated to bus duties in 1963, they were renumbered 849-852. SWN997 (1038) is captured here at Madera Drive, Brighton when it participated in the 1959 British Coach Rally.

The Llanelli 'New Dock' route required two new buses in 1959 to replace ageing stock. Normal under-floor engine buses were too high to pass beneath the low bridges of the district, one bridge having a clearance of only 9 feet. The AEC Regent V was the nearest approach to the old style front engine single decker's used on the service, so two Regent V's were specially bodied by C. H. Roe Coachworks, with low-height B37F single decker bodies as displayed here by TCY 102 (34). The sister vehicle was TCY 101 (33).

This is a rear view of TCY 102 (34) above, one of the unique Roe B37F bodied AEC Regent V's, and is seen in service at Burry Road, Machynys, Llanelli.

Even though carrying a 1959 registration number, TCY 663 was one of five AEC Reliance's delivered in 1962! TCY 662-4 (846-8) and TCY 665/6 (1821/2) formed a batch of Marshall B45F bodied Reliance's; with (1821/2) being chassis type 2MU2RA, Townhill buses. Seen here at Llanelli depot working Llanelli town service in 1971 is TCY 663, which was renumbered 253 in 1970.

UCY 837 (1203) was the first of another five AEC Bridgemaster's delivered in late 1959. Registered UCY 837-41 (1203-7) they were identical to the earlier five with Park Royal H41/31R bodies, and were the last rear entrance buses purchased new by the company. UCY 837 (1203), now in the care of Swansea Bus Museum, is undergoing a complete rebuild.

More AEC Reliance's arrived in 1960, in the form of VWN 11-15 (819-23), with Weymann B45F bodies. First of the batch, VWN 11 (819) is pictured here when new. They were renumbered 216-220 in 1970.

The major historical event of 1960, as far as SWT was concerned, occurred on the 5th January. The Mumbles Railway had been in decline for many years, at a time of rising costs, and it was revealed that £350,000 was needed to keep the line going. SWT received an act of Parliament for the dissolution of the Swansea & Mumbles Railway Ltd., and on 5th January 1960 the railway closed. In this view of cars No. 5 and 7, the
LMS railway line crosses Mumbles Road at Blackpill.

Oystermouth Station is the backdrop for this superb view of car No. 2. Each tramcar seated 106 passengers, and normally ran in pairs at peak times.
Note the SWT livery!

This two car train is seen leaving Oystermouth Station in 1959, led by car No. 4. The railway line followed the coastline of Swansea Bay for most of its journey, which was described as being exceptionally scenic. Note the amphibious DUKW on the beach

An interesting view of tramcar No.6 on Oystermouth Road, shows the Bay View Hotel in the background, with St. Helens Road going off to the left. The LMS railway line is captured on the right hand side, with the level crossing to Swansea beach and café. This view was taken from the footbridge which spanned Oystermouth Road and the LMS railway line – a crossing to the beach.

At busy times the Mumbles Railway tramcars operated in pairs coupled together, as seen from this view taken near Ashleigh Road Station on the Mumbles Road. The United Welsh 'Lodekka' appears to be racing the tramcars for passengers!

Even in its declining years, the Mumbles Railway had an unique appeal. When it was closed in 1960, the idea of preserving railways and working public transport systems was still almost unknown. Tramcar No.3 is seen here at Mumbles Pier terminus, with the lifeboat station visible on the left.

The Harrington Cavalier coachwork was widely regarded as one of the most attractive coach designs of the early sixties. Three were supplied to the company in 1960, built on AEC Reliance 2MU3RV chassis. They were registered VWN 16-18 (1042-4) and seated 37 passengers on Continental Tours. VWN 17 is seen here as an entrant in the 1960 British Coach Rally at Brighton. The company participated in this event for many years.

Fifteen AEC Regent V, 2D3RA models were purchased in 1960, all with Willowbrook H39/32F bodywork, 30 feet long. The batch were registered VWN 950-64 (534-548), and VWN 959 is seen here at Princess Way, Swansea, with rounded corners to the front mudguards. This batch of buses were the first to be so fitted, from new, to eliminate catching them in the bus wash. It was then adopted as standard by AEC, and the company modified the front mudguards on all other Regent's in the fleet.

Five more AEC Bridgemaster's arrived in early 1960, and were the first front entrance models built. Registered as WCY 888-92 (1208-12), their integral bodies, built by Park Royal seated 43 on the upper deck, and 29 on the lower deck. Last of the batch, WCY 892(1212) is pictured here when new.

The AEC Bridgemaster was developed in conjunction with BET companies that required low height double decker's. 60 MMD pictured here was an early prototype Bridgemaster with integral body structure built by Crossley Motors in 1958, a subsidiary of AEC Ltd. It was used as a demonstrator initially, and after spending two years as such was acquired by SWT in 1960 and painted into fleet livery, receiving fleet number 1213. It can be seen in full SWT livery on page 63.

XWN161 (1214), another AEC Bridgemaster with Park Royal H43/29F body was an 'odd one-out' just a single order. Built in 1960, it was exhibited at the 1960 Commercial Motor Show in Earls Court, and didn't enter service until 1961. Its seen here at Castle Street, Swansea, on its usual 'low-bridge' route to Port Tennant, a district to the east of Swansea.

Seen here on the forecourt of Neath depot (Eastland Road) in 1962 is XWN 812 (835), one of the 1961 batch of 2MU3RV type AEC Reliance's, XWN 801-22 (824-45), all fitted with Park Royal B45F bodies.

Two more Harrington Cavalier bodied AEC Reliance's arrived for the 1961 tours programme in the shape of YCY 295/6 (1045/6). They differed slightly from the earlier Harrington's having air brakes, opposed to vacuum. YCY 295 (1045) is seen here on the A76 road in Ayrshire, working a Scottish tour.

The last seven AEC Bridgemaster's were delivered in 1961, and were again built by Park Royal to H43/29F layout. This batch was registered YCY 795-801 (1215-21). In 1970, the company's remaining Bridgemaster's were renumbered, hence the fleet number 876 carried by YCY 797 when this view was taken at Princess Way (Castle Square), Swansea.

Castle Street (Castle Square), Swansea, is the backdrop to this view of YCY 806 (553), one of five more Willowbrook H39/32F bodied AEC Regent V's of 1961. The whole batch, YCY 802-6 (549-53) were renumbered 749-53 in 1970.

Captured here descending Penygraig Road, Townhill, in 1963 is YWN 121 (1819) one of a pair of AEC Reliance's with Park Royal B45F bodies delivered in 1961. This and YWN 122 (1820) were specially built for the Townhill route with AH470 engines fitted with dry sump lubrication
to prevent oil starvation on the hill, epicyclic gearboxes and air brakes.

The same chassis specification as above, 2MU2RA was carried by 403 BCY (1823) seen here carrying a heavy load on service 12 to Townhill. It was one of four special Townhill buses delivered in 1962, registered TCY 665/6, and 403/4BCY respectively. They received fleet numbers (1821-4) and were also fitted with Marshall B45F bodies.

The order for double decker's in 1962 amounted to twenty four AEC Regent V; 2D3RA models, all fitted with Willowbrook H39/32F bodywork. They were registered 989-999 BCY and 5-17 BWN with fleet numbers 554-77. First of the batch 989 BCY (554), later renumbered 754 is seen here at Kingsway roundabout in Swansea.

Willowbrook bodied AEC Regent V; 12 BWN (572) later renumbered 772, accompanied by ex. AEC demonstrator, 60 MMD (1213) an AEC Bridgemaster B3RA, with a rare Crossley H41/31R integral body. They are seen here together at Aberavon Beach coach park, probably on an excursion. 60 MMD (1213) is also pictured on page 60, as a demonstrator with the company

Although carrying a 1962 registration number, this AEC Reliance, 631 BWN (961) with Marshall B53F bodywork wasn't delivered until 1963 along with ten others in that year; 896-903 DCY, 631/2 BWN, and 732 FCY (953-63). They all had chassis type 2U3RA, with AH590 engines, synchromesh gearboxes, and were the first 36 feet long service buses in the fleet. They were all fitted with off-side illuminated advertising panels, a novelty of the 1960's. The location of this photo is the Cross Keys, Princess Way, Swansea.

Captured here at Tenby coach park on an excursion is 824 BWN (1047) another AEC Reliance 2MU3RA, with Harrington Cavalier C37F coachwork. It was one of the last two Cavalier's purchased by the company in 1962. This coach can now be seen in pristine condition at the Swansea Bus Museum.

On 1st September, 1962, the company absorbed the long established business of J. James & Sons Ltd., Ammanford, a fellow BET subsidiary. Thirty-five Leyland buses were taken into stock with the take-over, a mark that had left the company seven years earlier. Seen here inside Ammanford bus station (formerly James' depot) is a 1950 Leyland Titan PD2, which had been re-bodied in 1961 with a second-hand 1955 MCW 'Orion' body removed from a 1946 Leyland PS1 rebuild of James'.

Another Leyland from the James' fleet was this PSU1/13 Royal Tiger, with a horizontal Leyland 0.600 engine and Duple B44F body. New in 1952, it was one of four Royal Tiger's acquired with the James' take-over.

Six Leyland Tiger Cubs' were inherited from James Ammanford, this one NBX 77 (805) had a Weymann B44F body of true BET federation style. It is seen here inside the former James' depot about to depart for Swansea. The building in the background was originally a stable from the horse drawn carriage days of J. James & Sons.

MCW 'Orion' bodied Leyland 'Titan' PD2/12; NTH 33 (1222) was previously number 222 in the James' fleet. It is seen here at College Street, Ammanford having just pulled out of the Ammanford depot on route to Garnswllt. The building to the right was the staff canteen which was demolished in 1967 and replaced by the company's new Travel Agency shop, booking office and a new canteen upstairs.

The company acquired thirteen Leyland Atlantean's with the James' business in 1962, all fitted with the rare low-bridge bodywork by MCW and Weymann. Five of these are captured here at Church Street, Ammanford, on off-peak layover from the depot situated 100 yards away in Margaret Street/College Street. The leading vehicle RTH 637 (1227) was the first pre-production prototype 'Atlantean' to enter service in the world. Fitted with MCW, L39/34F bodywork, it was exhibited on the Leyland stand of the 1958 Commercial Motor Show in Earls Court, London.

Another former James Ammanford, Leyland Atlantean is seen leaving the erstwhile James' Bus Station at Ammanford. All the double decker's taken over with James' business were of low-bridge construction, a type that was essential in the Amman and Gwendraeth Valley area.
A detailed history of the James' business is still available from the publishers, at www.vernonmorgan.com

Pictured here at Aberavon Beach in the late 1960's is ex. James' Leyland Tiger Cub OBX 781 (808) a 1957 Weymann B44F bodied vehicle. This was the last single decker to enter James' fleet, and is still in existence today as a mobile caravan in the Bristol area – awaiting restoration to its former glory.

This was the vehicle exit to James' bus Station at College Street, Ammanford which became South Wales Transport's Ammanford depot in September 1962. The entrance to the depot was around the corner in Margaret Street. The double fronted house to the left of James' bus, RTH640 was James' office, previously John James the founder's residence. This is today the site of Ammanford bus station.

There were three Leyland Leopard PSU3/3R's on order at the time of James' merger in 1962. 894 DCY (951) pictured here at Church Street, Ammanford, was one of the trio ordered by James and delivered to SWT in 1963. Fitted with Marshall 53 seat bus bodies, it was a change of bodybuilder; in keeping with bodies already ordered for the delivery of eleven AEC Reliance's to SWT in 1963. 951 is seen here in 1969 displaying the new style of fleet-name.

One of the AEC Reliance's delivered to the company in 1963 was 896 DCY (953) with 2U3RA chassis and 36 feet long Marshall B53F bodies of BET federation design; incorporating off-side illuminated advertisement panels. They were all fitted with AH590 engines and synchromesh gearboxes, and registered 631/2 BWN; 896-903 DCY; 732 FCY (953-63).

A further six specially built AEC Regent V single decker's were built by Chas. Roe Coachworks in 1963, for the Llanelli 'New Dock' service. Identical to the unique pair delivered in 1959, they had chassis type 2D3RA, and were registered 279-284 DWN (35-40). They became 'redundant' in 1969 when most of the low bridges in New Dock were demolished, moving on to other depots. They were finally withdrawn and sold in 1972. No.38 has fortunately survived in preservation, and can be seen at the Swansea Bus Museum, in pristine condition.

The successor to the AEC 'Bridgemaster' was called the 'Renown', and based on a design using a separate chassis of low floor construction, conventional front axle and leaf springs, compared to the Bridgemaster's integral construction and independent front suspension. SWT was again early on the scene in regard to a new AEC model. 305 ECY (1242), seen here at Princess Way, Swansea, was one of the first batch of production chassis built. The first fourteen chassis ordered were bodied by Park Royal to a low floor design, with H39/32F layout, and delivered to the company in 1963. They were chassis type 3B3RA and registered 303-16 ECY with fleet numbers (1240-53).

A second batch of AEC Renown's arrived later in 1963, registered 534-8 FCY with fleet numbers (1254-8). Their chassis; type 3B3RA were numbered 001-5 indicating the first production chassis built, preceding 303-16 ECY (1240-53) received earlier. These bodies were built by Willowbrook to H39/32F layout, and looked quite similar to the Park Royal bodied examples delivered earlier.

Nine more AEC Regent V, type 2D3RA arrived in 1963 fitted with Willowbrook H39/32F bodywork. These were registered 146-54 FCY (578-86), later renumbered 778-86. Last of the batch, 154 FCY (586) is now preserved in pristine condition at the Swansea Bus Museum. Captured here at Old Castle Road, Llanelli, is 151 FCY (583) when still quite new.

732 FCY (963), another AEC Reliance 2U3RA with Marshall B53F body, was a solitary order delivered in 1963. It is seen here leaving the former James' bus station at Ammanford, working a former James' route to Swansea.

68

Captured here at Llanelli Town Hall Square, working route 26 to Morriston is 113 GWN (965), one of only three AEC Reliance 2U3RA's delivered in 1964, and again fitted with Marshall B53F bodies.

A further twenty AEC Regent V's were delivered to the company in 1964, but the order was split between 3 bodybuilders. Weymann bodied 420-8 HCY (587-95); with Park Royal bodying 429-33HCY (596-600), and Willowbrook bodying 434-9 HCY (601-6), all to H39/32F layout. This view of 428 HCY (595)was taken at Haverfordwest depot in September 1980, when it worked there branded with the 'Cleddau' name. The idea of using names with a local identity was widely adopted by the 'National Bus Company' in the 1979-1981 period. 'Cleddau' was a name adopted from the river Cleddau which flows through Pembrokeshire. Identical bus, 423 HCY (590) is now preserved, and owned by Swansea Bus Museum.

The 1965 intake of new vehicles was entirely AEC Regent V's. Numerically first of a batch of twenty-one was CCY 977C (607) pictured here when new. All the batch; CCY 977C-997C (607-27) had chassis type 2D3RA, fitted with AV590 engines and 27 feet long Willowbrook H37/27F bodies.

In 1966, a further thirteen AEC Regent V's arrived, registered GWN 856-866/8/70D (628-38/40//2) which was part of an order for eighteen. The remaining five were delivered in early 1967, and thus had 'E' suffix registrations; GWN 867/9E, GWN 871-3E (639/41/43-5). These all had Willowbrook H37/27F bodies as seen on GWN862D (renumbered 834 in 1970) captured here at Llanelli Town Hall Square, working a local service L14 to Penygraig Estate, complete with an advertisement for the local brew - 'Buckleys Beers'! From this batch, GWN 864D is awaiting restoration at the Swansea Bus Museum.

The last 'new' traditional style half-cab double decker's delivered to the company were AEC Regent V's GWN 867/9/71-3E (639/41/43-5) in 1967, as mentioned above. GWN 871E is seen here at Victoria Gardens, Neath, in 1973, in full National Bus Company (NBC) livery, having been re-numbered from 643 to 843 in 1970. The last Regent V ran for the company in 1982, marking the end of an era: 50 years of AEC Regent's. The last Regent to operate for the company, GWN 867E, is now in preservation, fully restored at Swansea Bus Museum.

After a lapse of 4 years, two more luxury coaches were added to the fleet in 1966. Again, the faithful AEC Reliance chassis was chosen. They were type 4U3RA with AH691, 11.3 litre engines, and fitted with 11 meter Plaxton Panorama C44F coachwork, the 'first' Plaxton's ever purchased. They were registered FWN 373/4D (1049/50). FWN 373D (1049) is photographed here at Brunswick Street depot, Swansea.

JWN 391E (1052) seen here when new was the second coach from a 1967 delivery. This and JWN 390E (1051) had AEC Reliance 8U3ZR chassis, with 6 speed ZF manual gearbox, and 11 meter coachwork, again by Plaxton, the 'Panorama', which seated 44.

In 1968 another pair of AEC Reliance 8U3ZR coaches arrived, identical to the previous delivery in 1967. These were registered NCY 296/7F (1053/4), and again had Plaxton Panorama C44F coachwork. In 1970, they were renumbered 170/1. NCY 297F (1054) is seen here on a Private Hire.

The entire 'bus' intake for 1968 consisted of AEC Reliance 6U2R models with AH691 engines. All fifteen buses were equipped with monocontrol semi-automatic transmission's; a type of vehicle that had previously only been purchased for the Townhill service. This was a major change in company policy. All were fitted with Willowbrook bodywork to BET federation design. NCY 284F (1953), one of the batch is pictured here when new, and is one of eight received before the change of registration prefix from F to G. They were NCY281-6/90/1F, NCY287-9/92-5G with fleet numbers (1950-64). All seated 53, except NCY289G (1958) which seated 52!

The 1969 intake of vehicles included twelve more AEC Reliance 6MU2R with the smaller AH505 engines, and semi-automatic transmission. Eight were B52F and four were dual purpose 49 seaters, all built by Marshall. PWN 967G (967) pictured here was first of the batch, and was fitted with 52 bus seats. The batch was registered PWN 967-78G (967-78). These were the first single decker's to receive the new style of livery, bright red with cream flashes below front and rear windows.

The first examples of yet another AEC model; the 'Swift' rear engined single decker arrived in 1969. They had chassis type 2MP2R, with AH505 engine of 8.2 litres. Registered PWN 701-3H (701-3), they were bodied by Willowbrook, with 48 seat front entrance and centre exit layout, and were equipped for one person operation. By mid-1971 the Swift's had been sold to London Country, a National Bus Company subsidiary. 702 is pictured here at Kingsway Roundabout in Swansea when new in 1969.

Only two coaches were purchased in 1969, and were the same chassis type as earlier deliveries of 1967/8; AEC Reliance 8U3ZR. However, they differed from the earlier ones in having Duple Northern 44 seat coachwork. They were registered RCY 55/6H (1055/6), renumbered 174/5 a year later. RCY 56H (1056) is seen here when new in 1969, on a tour to Ostend.

With the formation of the National Bus Company (NBC) in 1969 there were major changes within the company. The only new vehicles delivered in 1970 were four AEC Reliance 6U3ZR coaches with AH691 engines and ZF synchromesh gearboxes. Fitted with 44 seat Plaxton Panorama Elite coachwork, they were delivered unregistered with fleet numbers (1057-60). Immediately renumbered 176-9, they entered service with matching registration numbers XCY 176-9J, in 1970. 177 is seen here a few years later repainted into 'National' coach livery.

Nine AEC Regent V's with AV470 engines were received from City of Oxford Motor Services in 1969, in exchange for the thirteen ex. James of Ammanford, Leyland Atlanteans'. Oxford needed rear engine vehicles capable of one person operation to help overcome a severe staff shortage. The Regent's acquired from Oxford, 980/2-9 HFC (398, 92, 399, 94, 397, 396, 395, 98, 99), re-numbered 91-99 in 1970, were only operated for a year! 980 HFC (398), pictured here at Sketty Park Estate had a Willowbrook H37/26F body, as did the rest of the batch.

Acquired with the merger of Neath & Cardiff Coaches (N&C) of Briton Ferry in January 1971 was this 1958 AEC Reliance MU3RV with Weymann Fanfare C41F bodywork. RCY 805 pictured here, received fleet number 103 with SWT, and was withdrawn a few months later.

This Duple Northern bodied AEC Reliance 4MU3RA was also acquired with the N&C merger. New in 1965, CTX 985C received fleet number 158 with SWT, but was quickly transferred to Western Welsh O.C., as their 104. In March 1972 it returned to South Wales Transport as fleet number 158, together with Western Welsh's Haverfordwest depot, vehicles and services. As a point of interest, a former N&C Coaches, AEC Reliance (PTX 830F) with Plaxton coachwork, can be seen at the Swansea Bus Museum.

UCY 980J (461), an AEC Reliance 6MU2R with Plaxton DP49F coachwork was one of a pair ordered by SWT for N&C after SWT had taken control of N&C in 1969. This and UCY 979J were delivered in full N&C livery, with fleet numbers 979/80, becoming 460/1 in November 1970. It is seen here at Cardiff bus station in May 1978, working the former N&C, Cardiff – Swansea service by then extended beyond Swansea to reach Llanelli as route 252.

The company inherited forty-nine vehicles with the merger of Thomas Brothers, Port Talbot on 1st January 1971. This ex. Thomas Bros., 1957 Leyland Tiger Cub PSUC1/1, with Weymann B44F body, VTX 7, was numbered 309 with SWT.

Thomas Bros., also provided this 1965 AEC Reliance 4MU3RA with Weymann DP49F body. DNY 131C received fleet number 421, and is viewed here at the Sandfields estate in Port Talbot.

Ordered by Thomas Bros., Port Talbot before the merger with SWT were two Leyland PSUC1/12 Tiger Cub's with Marshall B45F bodies. They were delivered in full SWT livery after SWT had taken control in 1969, with 'Thomas Bros.' fleet-names. VTG 142G (325) pictured here at the original Haverfordwest bus station in July 1980, and its sister vehicle VTG 143G (326) were amongst the last Tiger Cub's to enter passenger service!

Painted into the National Bus Company's coach livery is HTG 179D (126) a 1966 AEC Reliance 2MU4RA, with manual transmission and Duple Northern C41F coachwork. This too came from the Thomas Bros., merger, and is seen here inside the former Thomas Bros., depot at Port Talbot.

Another smart Duple Commander C41F bodied AEC Reliance is seen here in 'National' coach livery. UWN 67H (134) had chassis type 6MU4R, and was ordered by Thomas Bros., before SWT took control of them in 1969. It was delivered to SWT in their livery of cream and red in 1970, named 'Afan Commander' and carrying Thomas Bros., fleet names, with fleet number 67. It was renumbered 134 in November 1970, and received SWT logo's.

The largest concern absorbed by South Wales Transport was that of Swansea based United Welsh Services in January 1970. Previously owned by the Transport Holding Company Ltd., United Welsh contributed 154 vehicles in the merger; 150 Bristol's and 4 Bedford's, the eldest being this 1956 Bristol LS6G, with ECW B45F body, MCY 40 (351), which is seen here at Princess Way, Swansea. It was withdrawn in 1973.

There were only two Bristol SUL4A's ever owned by United Welsh Services, and both had ECW C33F coachwork. New in 1962, they were registered 752/3 BWN and became numbers 120/1 with SWT. They were light-weight coaches, fitted with underfloor 4 cylinder Albion engines. 752BWN (120) is shown here in full SWT livery shortly before withdrawal in 1971

375 GWN (156) was a 1964 Gardner engined Bristol RELH6G with 47 seat ECW coachwork, inherited from United Welsh in the merger. This again was repainted into the SWT coach livery of the 1970 era. It can now be seen at the Swansea Bus Museum restored into its original United Welsh livery.

Pictured here at Brunswick Street depot, Swansea in June 1981 is KCY212E (166), another Bristol RELH6G with ECW C47F body. New in 1967, it was inherited from United Welsh in the merger. This Style of livery was used briefly in 1980/1 for vehicles operating 'Express' routes.

Captured here at Victoria Gardens, Neath, is one of the four Bedford VAM70's acquired from United Welsh. All four were fitted with Duple Viceroy C41F coachwork as seen here on UCY154H (132) in full SWT livery.

77

This Bristol MW6G was new to United Welsh as a 39 seat luxury coach in 1959. Acquired from United Welsh in the merger on 1st January 1970, it was one of many that were down-graded and converted into service buses by the company in 1971/2. Its ECW body was converted for one person operation by fitting power operated doors, bus type indicators, destination boxes and 45 second-hand bus seats. TWN 101 was given fleet number 372 in the single decker bus series, and is seen here at Llanelli Town Hall bus station.

Another Bristol MW6G acquired from United Welsh was WCY 705 (384) pictured here on route to Blaengwynfi. This was a standard Eastern Coachworks (ECW) bus bodied version with 45 seats.

Parked up on waste-land at Plymouth Street, Swansea, adjacent to the old United Welsh coach station is another ex. United Welsh Bristol MW6G with ECW B45F body. Registered 135ACY(387), and dating from 1961, it is seen here in full National Bus Company (NBC) bus livery of poppy red, with cream relief.

In its final years, United Welsh favoured single decker buses, and in particular the Bristol RE for most of the new vehicles placed in service. This RELL6G with ECW 54 seat body was one of a batch of seven dating from 1965, but a total of twenty-two basically similar RE's were among the vehicles transferred to SWT.

This Bristol RELL6G, SCY463G (620) was yet another RE acquired from United Welsh. Dating from 1969, it was fitted with ECW B53F bodywork and is seen here at Lammas Street, Carmarthen in full NBC livery, working the 105 Carmarthen to Swansea service via Tumble, Cross Hands and Pontarddulais.

Ordered by United Welsh in 1969, but delivered direct to SWT in 1972 were three Bristol RELL6G's with ECW B53F bodies; DCY 410-2K (648-50). They were the balance of an order for eight such vehicles, the other five entered service in 1971 as XWN 623/4J (623/4) and ACY 640-2K (640-2). DCY 410K (648) is seen here at Plymouth Street, Swansea.

Seventy-five Bristol Lodekka's were inherited with the United Welsh merger in January 1971. Seen here is one of the earlier examples; SWN 155 (912) a Bristol LD6G with ECW H33/27R body dating from 1959. It is pictured here carrying an experimental style fleet name in March 1972, which was similar to the one carried on coaches.

Another Bristol LD6G 'Lodekka from the same 1959 batch that passed into SWT ownership was SWN 158 (915). It is seen here at Old Castle Road, Llanelli in 1972, at the terminus of service 2 to Swansea. This service had previously been jointly operated between SWT and United Welsh. SWN 159 (916), another LD6G from the same batch is in preservation, converted to open top at the Swansea Bus Museum

The Bristol 'Lodekka' was Bristol's answer to a low height double decker, which incorporated a low entrance, low floor and a centre gangway on the upper deck. 148 ACY (947), a 1961 Bristol FSF6G 'Lodekka' with ECW H34/26F body was another vehicle received from United Welsh in the merger. The Lodekka's, 141-53 ACY (940-52) were United Welsh's first front entrance double decker's in 1961.

268 DCY (963) was another short length, front entrance Bristol FSF6G (Gardner engined) Lodekka transferred from United Welsh. New in1962, this was also bodied by ECW as H34/26F, and is viewed here at Victoria Gardens bus station, Neath.

Captured here at Victoria Gardens, Neath, in full NBC livery is a long chassis version of the Bristol Lodekka. New to United Welsh in 1964, 132 FCY (977) was designated chassis type FLF6G and fitted with ECW (Eastern Coachworks) H38/32F body – the standard body for THC group companies, of which United Welsh was a member. It was one of nine FLF6G's (970-8) delivered to United Welsh in 1963/4.

A delivery of twelve new AEC Swift (2MP2R) buses with Marshall B53F bodywork had barely entered service with the company in 1971 before they were transferred to NBC subsidiary London Country. Seen here before departure to London is XCY 469J (469) at Llanelli Town Hall Square bus station, during its short stay in South Wales. The batch registered XCY 462-73J, had matching fleet numbers 462-73

81

The only other intake of 'new' vehicles in 1971 were those which had been ordered by the companies that merged with SWT. YWN 553J (261), seen here at Port Talbot was ordered by Thomas Bros., of Port Talbot, but delivered direct to SWT in their livery. The batch of three YWN 553/5/6 (261/3/2) were AEC Reliance type 6MU2R, with Willowbrook B45F bodies.

The Bristol RE pictured here at Plymouth Street, Swansea, was one of eight (623/4/40-2/8-50) ordered by United Welsh before the merger in 1970. This Bristol RELL6G, ACY 641K (641) with Eastern Coachworks B53F body was one of the second batch, ACY 640-2K delivered in 1971. The third batch, DCY 410-2K (648-50) arrived in 1972, and all were delivered in full SWT (NBC) livery.

To cover the interval between the transfer of the fifteen AEC Swifts to London Country in June 1971, and the arrival of fifteen replacement vehicles; diverted Bristol RELL6L's from Western Welsh Omnibus Co. (NBC) in late 1971, fourteen elderly Leyland 'Olympian' and 'Tiger Cubs' were borrowed from Western Welsh. LKG 219 (333), a Leyland Olympian with Weymann B44F body, seen here on Middle Road, Swansea, was one of seven that were taken into stock by SWT two months later in August 1971

The fifteen Bristol RELL6L's mentioned on the previous caption were ordered by, and delivered to, Western Welsh in 1971, but none entered service with that company. They were immediately transferred to SWT to replace the fifteen AEC Swifts sent to London Country in June 1971. UKG 811J (630), seen here, was one of the fifteen. Registered UKG806-20J (625-39), they all had Marshall 51 seat bodywork of BET style.

After the formation of NBC in 1970, there was an acute shortage of buses within the company, caused by short term operational needs until service patterns could be rationalised. This brought about an intake of second-hand vehicles from other NBC subsidiaries. The first seventeen were elderly Bristol MW6G's acquired from Royal Blue, with 39 seat ECW coach bodies. These were converted into 45 seat buses (as were the ex. United Welsh MW6G's) using bus seats destination boxes and power operated doors before entering service in 1972. Former Royal Blue (Western National) 2228, XUO 711 seen here at Kingsway, Swansea, was one of the first converted, and received fleet number (264).

Another second-hand vehicle in 1971 was this 1958 Bristol LD6G 'Lodekka' with ECW, H33/25RD body. 261 HNU (908) seen here, was acquired from Midland General O.C. (NBC subsidiary) together with identical 260 HNU (907) and a rare Bristol LDL6G, with ECW H37/33RD body registered 13 DRB (906).

83

Old Castle Road, Llanelli, is the backdrop for this view of the last AEC Reliance bus purchased by the company. BWN 466K (466) was numerically the last of the batch; BWN 462-6K (462-6) delivered in November 1971. Entering service in 1972, they had 6MU2R type chassis with Marshall DP49F bodies, and received fleet numbers that were previously carried by the AEC Swifts transferred to London Country. It's seen working a Llanelli local service, 172 to the British Leyland car factory at Felinfoel, in February 1972.

Besides the five Reliance's mentioned above, the only other intake of new vehicles in 1972 were three Bristol RELL6G's with ECW, B53F bodies, DCY 410-2K (648-50) which were ordered by United Welsh before the merger. DCY 411K (649) is seen here at Singleton Street, Swansea, working a service to the small picturesque village of Rhossili on the western tip of the Gower Peninsular.

A further fifteen Bristol MW and LS coaches with ECW bodies were acquired in 1972, and rebuilt into one person operated buses, as mentioned earlier. 614 JPU (282) seen here at Neath railway station, was a 1957 Bristol LS6G with ECW C39F body converted to DP45F. It was previously owned by City of Oxford Motor Services, another NBC subsidiary.

WKG 277 (257), a 1961 AEC Reliance 2MU3RA with Willowbrook DP41F body was acquired on 1st January 1970, together with an assortment of 35 vehicles, and the Neath Abbey depot of Western Welsh Omnibus Co. This was purely an amalgamation of W.W.O.C. services, as they too were part of the NBC.

On 27th March 1972, the company absorbed the services of Western Welsh at Haverfordwest, in another rationalisation plan! An assortment of twenty-one Leyland's and one AEC were acquired here, together with the services and depot. SBO 248 (303) a 1959 Leyland PSUC1/1 Tiger Cub pictured here with Park Royal B43F body was one of the vehicles received from W.W.O.C. in the Haverfordwest take-over.

Another Leyland Tiger Cub transferred with the Western Welsh Haverfordwest depot and services in March 1972 was 300 CUH (345), a PSUC1/11 with B45F Marshall body. New in 1963, it had fleet number 1300 with W.W.O.C. and is captured here at Tenby, working ex. W.W.O.C. service 308 to Saundersfoot. In 1978 it was converted into a towing bus and painted bright Yellow. When finally withdrawn in 1985, the registration number was transferred to a new 'Neoplan' double decker coach.

HBO 394D (340) was
another Leyland Tiger
Cub acquired from
Western Welsh but
came via the Neath
Abbey transfer, even
though it is seen here,
working   at
Haverfordwest.   340
had   chassis   type
PSUC1/12   and   a
Marshall B43F body.

Two more ex. Western
Welsh buses are
photographed here in
September 1980, at
Haverfordwest depot.
KKG 213F (213) an AEC
Reliance 6MU3R with
Marshall DP41F body in
full NBC dual purpose
livery, and PKG 629G
(508) a Leyland
PSU3A/4R Leopard with
Marshall B51F body are
withdrawn and await their
fate. 213 also came via the
Neath Abbey transfer.

The buses transferred to
SWT with the Western
Welsh's Neath Abbey depot
included the remaining five
1971 Bristol RELL6L's with
Marshall B51F bodies: UKG
801-5J   (643-7).   The
company   had   already
received fifteen of this
batch, UKG 806-20 (625-
39) diverted from W.W.O.C.
when new in 1971. UKG
804J (646) is viewed here at
Victoria Gardens, Neath, in
1978.

Four Leyland PDR1/3 Atlantean's with Northern Counties H41/32 F bodies passed over to SWT with the take-over of Haverfordwest depot. They were all 1969 models, PKG 367/374-6H (901-4), one of which is seen here at Haverfordwest depot; PKG 375H (903) previously fleet number 375 with Western Welsh.

Additionally, five former United Automobile Services (NBC subsidiary), Bristol MW6G's with ECW, C39F bodies; 4206-10 HN were acquired 1972. They were similarly converted into 45 seat buses, as were the earlier purchases of second - hand MW6G coaches. Pictured here is 4209 HN (294) in NBC all over red livery, a livery introduced in August 1972. This MW had however, been fitted with a replacement driver's windscreen at some point.

Adding to the long list of second-hand purchases in 1972, were eleven more Bristol MW6G's with ECW B45F bodies from Red & White Services, Chepstow. Dating from 1957, SWO 97 (259) seen here was one of the bunch acquired. It was renumbered 559 in 1974, shortly before withdrawal, to make way for incoming new Ford R1014's numbered in the 2xx series.

Over a period of nine years, the company built up a fleet of 121 'new' Leyland National buses, and acquired several second hand examples. The first batch of these integrally built buses delivered in 1973, LWN701-13L (701-13) were 11.3 meter, 52 seater's fitted with the Leyland 510 engine of 8.2 litre capacity. Seen here operating from Haverfordwest depot when new is LWN706L (706). A second batch of identical Leyland National's arrived later in 1973 registered NWN714-28M (714-28).

Additions to the coach fleet in 1973 took a rather less predictable turn, with a chassis make not previously purchased by the company. This was a Bedford YRT with Willowbrook 002, C51F coachwork, registered PCY909M (509), which is seen here at Cardiff bus station, operating the former N&C Coaches express service from Swansea to Cardiff.

Further examples of 'lightweight' buses delivered in 1973 were nine Bedford YRQ's with Willowbrook Expressway C45F bodies; PWN219-27M (219-27). Captured here at Haverfordwest depot in September 1980 is Bedford YRQ, PWN222M (222), in the NBC poppy red and white dual purpose livery, complete with 'Cleddau' branding, a local identity name for Haverfordwest based vehicles.

Another 'first' chassis manufacture entered the fleet in 1974, when the company purchased thirty-five new Ford R1014, 10 meter buses. The model featured a lightweight chassis with front engine layout, manual gearboxes, and all fitted with Willowbrook B45F bodies. Registered PWN228-37M, RWN238-47M, SWN86/7M, SWN249/50/2M, TCY253-62M, they carried fleet Nos., (228-62) respectively. PWN231M, seen here at Swansea, had matching fleet number 231.

This Ford R1014, SWN87M (251) was delivered as RWN251M, with matching fleet number 251, but entered service in 1974 as SWN87M. It is seen here at Tenby multi-storey car park about to depart on route 308 to Saundersfoot, a service inherited from Western Welsh in March 1972.

Another Ford R1014 from the 1974 delivery was TCY257N (257), which is seen here at Coracle Way, Carmarthen.

Only three AEC Reliance's were purchased in 1974, all with type 6U3ZR chassis; featuring 6 speed ZF manual gearboxes and Duple Dominant l, 49 seat coach bodies. Registered TCY180M, UCY181/2N (180-2), they were the penultimate AEC's purchased by the company.

A further twenty-five 11.3 meter Leyland National's arrived in 1974, numbered 729-53. TCY732M (732) is captured here leaving the former United Welsh Services coach station into Princess Street, Swansea. The Volunteer Arms is just visible in this view; a landmark demolished along with Princess Street, yet the coach station remains; now converted into a shop for Wilkinsons.

Another Leyland National; type 11351/1R, 52 seater, GCY744N (744) is pictured here at the newly opened Quadrant Bus Station, Swansea, in 1980.

Seen here at the former Ammanford outstation (Capel Hendre Industrial Estate) on 5th May 1985, is TWN749N (749) another 1974 Leyland National, which was registered out of sequence.

The last Leyland National delivered in 1974 was GCY753N (753), seen here at Neath railway station on 31st October, 1987, by then owned by the 'Privatised' South Wales Transport Co, as seen by the logo on the front of the bus.

Delivered in full NBC dual purpose livery in 1975 was TWN466N (467) another AEC Reliance 6U2R with Duple Dominant 1, C49F body. Captured here when new, at Cardiff bus station, working the 252 Cardiff – Swansea service, it was a service inherited from N&C, and extended to reach Llanelli. This bus was quickly re-registered HCY467N (467), into the series of a later delivery.

After a span of 56 years, the long association with AEC came to an end in 1975, with delivery of the company's last new AEC's. Registered TWN466N, later to HCY467N (see above) and HCY468-71N (467-71) they were all 6U2R Reliance's with semi-automatic transmission and Duple Dominant 1 coach bodies finished to dual purpose standards as shown here by HCY468N.

Purchased by the company in September 1974, in a damaged condition, was this former Eastern National O.C., 1953 Bristol KSW5G, WNO484 (500) with ECW, OT33/28R body. Repaired using parts from former United Welsh KSW6G breakdown wagon, HWN339, it entered service in May 1975 on the scenic route to Mumbles. After spending twenty-two years with the company, operating in many liveries, it now resides at the Swansea Bus Museum – in full United Welsh livery!

JTH767P (767), a Leyland National 11351/1R, 52 seater was one of a batch registered JTH754-86P (754-86) and delivered in 1975-6. 767 was licenced in 1976, and is seen here at Llanelli depot on 24th August, 1986.

Port Talbot depot is the backdrop for this view of JTH777P (777), another Leyland National 11351/1R from the 1976 delivery. It's seen here carrying the 'Afanway' branding, a local identity name for Port Talbot area buses, a name derived from the river Afan which passes through the town.

This 1962 AEC Reliance 4MU4RA with Marshall B53F body, 773 NJO (400), was acquired from City of Oxford M.S., in 1975. It only operated briefly, and is seen here at Ravenhill depot after withdrawal in 1976.

The second and final batch of Ford R1014's arrived in 1976, and were all fitted with Duple Dominant B43F bodies. First of the batch, NCY 263R (263) is seen here at Port Talbot bus station carrying the Port Talbot area branding 'Afanway'. The idea of using names with a local identity for bus services was widely adopted by NBC in the 1979-81 period.

NCY 268R (268) was one of the batch of seventeen Ford R1014's mentioned above, delivered in 1976 as NCY 263-79R (263-79). It carries the standard NBC bus livery of the period.

When the Duple bodied Ford R1014's (263-79) were withdrawn from passenger service in 1983, NCY 266/71/7R (266/71/7) were shortened by 3 feet in length and converted into tow-buses, as shown here by NCY 277R (277) parked at Haverfordwest depot on 18th July, 1987.

The first Leyland Leopard's to be ordered by the company were five with PSU3C/4R type chassis, and Duple Dominant Express, C49F coachwork, NCY 472-6R (472-6). They were delivered in 1976, in full NBC red and white dual purpose livery. First of the batch NCY 472R (472) is seen here at the old Carmarthen bus station on 15th August, 1984, in a special dual purpose livery and original style 'South Wales' fleet-name, working the short lived 'Express West' 611 service, Bristol – Haverfordwest. Additionally, it had been renumbered 164, in the new fleet numbering series.

NCY 475R (originally number 475) from the same batch of Leopard's mentioned above, is seen here entering the Swansea 'Quadrant' bus station on 21st July, 1987, after the company had been 'privatised' by a management buy-out in May 1987. It had quickly received the new livery of lime green, leaf green and white, with red relief, and the new style SWT logo. It had also been re-numbered 167 in the new coach series.

Two more Leyland Leopard's arrived in 1977. Registered RWN 477/8S (477/8), they had chassis type PSU3E/4R; semi-automatic, and again were fitted with Duple Dominant, C49F coachwork. They were delivered in full NBC red and white dual purpose livery, as seen here on RWN 477S (477) at Cardiff bus station on 22nd October 1977.

Also seen at Cardiff bus station, working the former N&C Express service; by then extended to Llanelli as service 252 is RWN 478S (478). New in 1977, it was another Leyland Leopard PSU3E/4R with Duple Dominant C49F body.

In 1976, the company acquired three new Leyland Leopard's transferred from NBC subsidiary, Midland Red without entering service there. Registered by Midland Red as JOX 441-3P, they were 1976 Leyland Leopard PSU3C/4R, with Plaxton Panorama Supreme III, C47F coachwork, and were given fleet numbers 183-5. JOX 443P (185) is seen here when new, in full National Express livery. It was later re-registered MKH 644A, and fitted with a new Plaxton Panorama Supreme V front end, modernising its looks.

One of the first Bristol VRT's delivered to the company in 1976 was OCY 906R (906) pictured here on lay-over at the old Carmarthen bus station on 31st October, 1984. The batch delivered late 1976, early 1977 were Leyland 501 engined, OCY 905-16R (905-16). Fitted with ECW, H43/31F bodies they were the first 'new' double decker's in the fleet for ten years. 906 here was re-bodied by ECW in 1981 after the original body was destroyed by fire, and was later re-numbered 998 to accommodate incoming Leyland Olympian's No's 901-7.

Out-stationed at Scurlage (Gower), is Gorseinon based; ECW bodied Bristol VRT, RTH 918S (918) which was new in 1977. The company purchased a total of 91 'new' Bristol VRT's through the years, all fitted with Leyland 501 engines – the same unit as the Leyland National's, but vertically mounted.

Three convertible open-top buses were purchased new in 1977, for use on the summertime Swansea-Mumbles-Langland and Caswell Bay service's 71,72 and 73. The vehicles concerned RTH 930-2S (930-2) were Bristol VRT/SL3/501's, with ECW, COH43/31F bodies, as seen in this view of RTH 930S, in its original livery of poppy red and white.

RTH 931S (931) was numerically the second detachable top Bristol VRT from the 1977 delivery of three open-topper's. Their roofs' were only removed for a few weeks during the season and worked most of the year with covered top's fitted, as shown here by 931 at Brunswick depot in February 1979.This bus was amongst the first batch of vehicles delivered with the bi-lingual fleet-name, 'De Cymru' on the off-side, a practice that continued on the rest of the fleet during the winter, 1977-8

In 1989, SWT repainted one of the Bristol VRT convertible open-top's into the original South Wales Transport livery to celebrate the company's 75th anniversary. RTH 931S (931) was the vehicle chosen for the special occasion, and is seen here at Margam Country Park on 25th June, 1989, carrying out 75th anniversary celebrations with free rides around the park. This bus is now awaiting restoration at the Swansea Bus Museum.

Another view of the convertible open-top Bristol VRT., RTH 931S (931) is shown here with its top fitted. All three convertibles were later named after famous local people. 930-2 became 'Dylan Thomas' 'Harry Seacombe' and 'John H Vivian' respectively. However, the 'lids' of 930/932 were interchanged after one summer season, resulting in them carrying the wrong name-plates.

One of the Leyland National's from the 1977 delivery is OEP 788R (788) a 52 seater from a batch of ten, registered OEP787-96R (787-96). Its seen here at Castle Street, Swansea when new.

Mini-buses first appeared with the company in 1977, when two vehicles that had previously been operated by City of Oxford Motor Services (NBC subsidiary) were acquired for use on a new 'Gower Pony' service. NWL 704M (98), new in 1973 was a diesel engined Ford Transit, with a 16 seat conversion of the parcel van body carried out by Strachan Coachworks. It's seen here at the company's Clarence Terrace depot, Swansea, on 15th December, 1979.

Seven more Leyland National's arrived in 1978. Seen here at Capel Hendre out station is Leyland National 11351A/1R, TWN 797S (797); another 52 seater, single door layout model, which was numerically first in the batch. They were registered TWN797-9S, WEP800T, TWN 801-3S (797-803).

Due to the late delivery of Leyland National No. 800 in 1978, it lost its allocated registration number of TWN 800S, and received a new number WEP 800T, in keeping with its first licencing date; August 1978. WEP 800T (800) is seen here at Cardiff bus station, working an express service to Brecon.

The company introduced the 'Cityrunner' X11 service between Burry Port and Swansea in September 1990. It was introduced initially to retaliate against Davies Bros.(Pencader) Ltd's introduction of a new direct Llanelli to Swansea service numbered 666. Note the Davies Bros, '666' bus stop sign on top of the bus shelter! Leyland National TWN 803S (803) was specially branded for the Cityrunner service

This pair of standard ECW, H43/31F bodied Bristol VRT's, TWN 933S/WTH 952T (933/952) were delivered in 1978 and 1979 respectively, and were captured here at Llanelli depot on 1st February, 1987, just three months before the company was 'de-nationalised'; purchased by the management team, D.Bending, A.D.Kreppel, G.Turley and I.Moore. The advertisement on the side of the bus for a return, Swansea to London at £13.00 sounds reasonable, but Eynon's of Trimsaran were offering a Llanelli to London return at £5.00 in 1987.

Advertising on buses has always paid the operators good revenue. In the late 1970's, it became commonplace to see buses painted in various all over advertising liveries, as displayed by this South Wales Transport, ECW bodied Bristol VRT, TWN 936S (936), seen entering Swansea 'Quadrant' bus station, carrying an all over advertisement for Sainsbury's Swansea store, on 15th February 1986.

Swansea 'Quadrant' bus station is where Bristol VRT, VTH 942T (942) was photographed in 1980. It's typical of the once large number of ECW bodied Bristol VRT's operated by SWT. After withdrawal it passed to Western National in Somerset. The vehicle is now in preservation at the Swansea Bus Museum, carrying the livery of Western National.

Haverfordwest depot is the backdrop for this view of another 1978 Bristol VRT, WTH 945T (945). It displays the 'Cleddau' branding;
a local identity name for the Haverfordwest services, together with the NBC logo. Considering the view was taken on 24th May 1987, sixteen days after de-nationalisation, the NBC logo hadn't been removed, yet the new SWT logo had been applied to the front. This particular batch of ECW bodied VRT's were registered WTH 944-62T (944-62), of which WTH 961T (961) is now fully restored in Swansea Bus Museum.

WWN 806T (806) was one of six type 11351A/1R Leyland National 52 seaters' delivered in 1979, and is photographed here at Swansea Quadrant bus station shortly after it opened in 1979. The Building in the left-hand background is the former United Welsh Services coach station, which was still operational at that time. It's now converted into the Wilkinsons store.

The final six Leyland National l, type 11351A/1R delivered in 1979 were registered AWN 810-5V (810-5). The penultimate Leyland National Mk l, AWN 814V (814) is seen here at the Quadrant bus station, Swansea, on a lay-over in 1981. Sister vehicle, AWN 813V (813) is now at the Swansea Bus Museum awaiting restoration.

The company were amongst early recipients of the Leyland National Mk 2, receiving five examples in 1980, registered CCY 816-20V (816-20). The Mk 2's were fitted with Leyland 680 engines and had a slightly increased length, to 11.6 meters, seating 52 when new, later re-seated to DP48F. CCY 820V (820), pictured here entering Swansea Quadrant bus station on 27th February 1986 was the penultimate Mk 2 delivered, the last one KEP829X (829) arrived in 1982. CCY 820V is now in preservation at the Swansea Bus Museum.

A further twenty-four Bristol VRT's were delivered in early 1980, registered as BEP 963-86V (963-86). These again were the standard Bristol VRT/SL3/501 models with ECW, H43/31F bodies as seen here on BEP 977V (977) at Llanelli depot on 24th August 1986. Sister vehicle, BEP 978V is now awaiting restoration at the Swansea Bus museum.

Bristol VRT ECY 991V (991) is seen here at the old Carmarthen bus station on 3rd August 1983, working the first part of the 'Express West' service to Bristol. It was one of the final batch of Bristol VRT's delivered in 1980, which were registered ECY 987-991V/EWN 992-5V (987-95).

No less than twelve second hand Leyland National Mk l's were taken into stock in 1981 from NBC subsidiary, East Kent. One of them, NFN 78M (827) an 11.3 meter version is seen here at Carmarthen bus station on 26th September, 1984 working the Ammanford to Carmarthen service 129. Eight Nationals' were also acquired from London Country, another NBC subsidiary, in 1982.

Only six Leyland National Mk 2's were purchased by the company. The last one, delivered in 1981, KEP 829X (829), model/type NL116AL11/1R is seen here in full NBC dual purpose livery entering Swansea Quadrant bus station on 15th February, 1986. It was 11.6 meters long, and fitted with 44 dual purpose seats and a Leyland 680 engine.

Leyland National Mk 1, NPD 136L (835) was one of eight acquired from London Country in 1982. This 11.3 meter version is seen here leaving Ammanford bus station on 20th November 1983, accompanied by a Rees & Williams' Leyland Leopard. Ammanford bus station was originally James, Ammanford's bus station. John James had acquired this premises in 1900, operating ponies and trap's from here when it was known as Brynderwen Mews. The buses are standing on the area previously occupied by John James' house! A detailed history of the James' business is still available from the publisher at:www.vernonmorgan.com

Another second-hand Leyland National Mk 1 acquired in 1982 was GFN 551N. Numbered in a new series as 351, it was acquired from East Kent in the batch of twelve mentioned earlier. This was a 41 seat 10.3 meter model and is seen here on 17th October 1983 at Ammanford bus station. The building being erected in the background is the Co-operative store.

104

Captured here at SWT's Neath depot yard (former Western Welsh depot) on 17th March 1979, is a former Trent (NBC), Leyland Leopard, Plaxton Panorama 45 seat coach, PRC 210F (171) in full NBC dual purpose livery. It was one of a pair, PRC 209/10F obtained for the newly acquired Landore Park & Ride service.

This Leyland Leopard PSU3E/4RT with Willowbrook 003 Express; 51 seat body was one of three delivered in early 1980 in all over white livery, but received the red band shown before entering service. BTH 481V (481) seen here was later re-numbered 173, in a series for coaches. The registration index mark TH, previously issued by Carmarthenshire C.C., was by now issued by Swansea LVL Office, since the re-allocation of index marks associated with the local government re-organisation in 1974.

The 'Express West' limited stop service linking Swansea and Bristol via Port Talbot, Cardiff and Newport, via the M4 motorway was introduced on 19th September, 1981, and ran jointly with Bristol Omnibus Co., and National Welsh. A special livery was used for this service as shown here on BTH 483V (175, originally No.483) another Willowbrook 003 Express bodied Leyland Leopard as above. By the time this view was taken in March 1984, the service had been extended to Llanelli, Carmarthen and Haverfordwest.

Due to the amazing success of the 'Gower Pony' minibus service introduced in 1977, two new Bedford CFL, 17 seaters, CEP196/7V (96/7) with Reeve Burgess bodywork were purchased in 1980 to replace the aging Ford Transit's. Here CEP197V (97) is seen in full NBC poppy red livery entering Swansea bus station, displaying the Gower Pony branding, which had also been carried by the earlier Transit's.

In April 1981, the activities of National Travel (South West) at Swansea were transferred to SWT. Twenty-three vehicles, all Leyland Leopards' were absorbed in the merger. Amongst them was KAD 344V pictured here, a 1980, 12 meter Leyland Leopard PSU5C/4R, with Plaxton Supreme IV, 57 seat coachwork. This was given fleet number 155.

In the early 1980's, Plaxton Coachworks offered re-furbishment deals on their Supreme III bodies. The offer included re-upholstered seats, new floor covering and a modern new Supreme V front end fitted, as seen here on MKH 622A (183). Repainted in National Holidays livery, MKH 622A, was originally registered JOX 441P; a Leyland Leopard transferred from Midland Red when new in 1976; carrying NBC coach livery of all over white.

MKH 733A (184), originally registered JOX 442P was another ex. Midland Red Leyland Leopard, Plaxton Supreme III that was re-furbished in the 1980's, and fitted with a Supreme V front end. It's seen here at Swansea Quadrant bus station on 17th April 1988, a year after privatisation of the company, wearing a new 'Days Away' livery. It was sold for scrap in February 1993 after a brief spell working for SWT's associate company 'Brewers'.

One of the eldest coaches inherited from the National Travel (South West) merger in 1981 was this 1972 Leyland Leopard, FDF 342L (187) with Duple Dominant I body. It's seen here entering Swansea bus station.

Seen here at Carmarthen bus station on Christmas eve 1986 is MKH 748A (195), another ex. National Travel (South West) Leyland PSU5C/4R Leopard with Duple Dominant II, C51F coachwork dating from 1979. Originally registered GDF 281V, it's captured here working the 'Express West' 612 service to Bristol.

More lightweight vehicles arrived in 1980/1, but this time on Bedford YMQ chassis with Allison automatic transmission. There were eighteen in all, registered FCY 280-97W (280-97) all fitted with Duple Dominant bus type bodywork. The first seven had high backed dual purpose seating for 45 passengers, the remainder had 43 bus seats, with luggage pens, as seen here on FCY 293W (293), at Capel Hendre out-station in August 1985.

In 1984, the seven dual purpose seated Bedford YMQ's mentioned above FCY 280-6W (280-6) were re-painted into a new d/p livery identical to the one carried by some of the Duple Dominant and Willowbrook 003, bodied Leyland Leopard's. These Bedford's however had the branding of 'Countryside Explorer' added, as displayed here on 280.

Another Bedford YMQ from the same batch as above was FCY 296W, fitted with 43 bus seats. It is seen here at Carmarthen bus station in full NBC livery and Haverfordwest branding 'Cleddau', working the Haverfordwest – Bristol, 'Express West' service on 24th October, 1984.

The last batch of Willowbrook 003, bodied Leyland PSU3F/4R Leopard's, LCY 101-10X (101-10) were delivered in 1981-2. The first eight had C49F seating whilst the last two were C46F. Originally purchased for the 'Express West' service, LCY 106X (106) pictured here in 1991, had been re-painted into the 'Cityrunner' livery to work the X11 Llanelli-Swansea service, challenging Davies Bros' similar service '666'. 101-108 had 'Express' type bodies.

The penultimate Willowbrook 003, delivered to the company LCY 109X (109), is seen here on 15th August, 1984, in full National Express livery, working the 'Express West' 610 service to Cardigan. This coach seated 46 passengers, and had a coach type entrance doorway, as did 110.

To replace the AEC Regent's on service 14, five Bedford YMQS's with specially shortened chassis were purchased in order to negotiate a sharp bend at Plough Corner, near Pennard. They had Lex Maxata 37 seat bodywork as shown here by LCY 302X (302) soon after entering service in February, 1982. The five were registered LCY298-302X (298-302) and became redundant in 1984 when a road improvement took away the notorious corner. LCY 299X is now at the Swansea Bus museum awaiting restoration.

The last five new Leyland Leopard's delivered to the company in 1982 had PSU5E/4R type, 12 meter chassis, fitted with Duple Dominant IV Express, C53F bodies. The batch was registered MCY 111-6X (111-6), of which, 115 is seen here leaving Carmarthen bus station working the 'Express West' 611 service to Haverfordwest, in National Express livery, on 24th October 1984. It was later re-registered MKH 678A.

In 1983, the National Express 'Rapide' network of services called for a higher specification type of coach. As a result, SWT placed five Leyland Tiger TL11 engined coaches in service, with Duple Caribbean high spec., 46 seat bodies, featuring refreshment and toilet facilities, and finished to 'Rapide' standards. They were registered RCY117-21Y, with matching fleet numbers 117-21. RCY 119Y (119) is seen here working the 506 service from Haverfordwest to London on 25th April 1984. It was later re-registered MKH 896A.

Another Leyland Tiger from the same batch as above is seen here at Swansea bus station in 1983, working the 505 service, Swansea to London. The 505 service was later extended to Llanelli on some journeys. RCY 121Y (121) viewed here was re-registered MKH 48A in 1985.

One of the second batch of
Leyland Tiger's with 260bhp
TL11 engines and Duple
Caribbean bodies was A125
XEP (125), seen here on 18th
July, 1984. The batch
registered   A122-5
XEP/A126 WEP (122-6),
and delivered in 1984 were
identical to the five
delivered in 1983. 125 was
later re-registered MKH
89A. The final four
Tiger/Duple Caribbean's
arrived in 1985 with
registration No's B127-30
CTH (127-30).

The delivery of new vehicles came to a standstill in the mid
1980's, and quite a number of second hand buses and
coaches were taken into stock. Amongst them was this
Bristol VRT with ECW body from Alder Valley, a NBC
subsidiary. Registered TPE 152S (996) it is seen here out-
stationed at Scurlage from Gorseinon depot on 21st July,
1985. This and VRT, TPE 153S (997) were acquired from
Alder Valley in exchange for the five short Bedford
YMQS's that had become 'redundant' in 1984. Although
being identical in appearance to the ninety-one VRT's
purchased new by SWT, they differed in having Gardner
6LXB engines.

UFM   37F   (503)
pictured   here   at
Swansea bus station
was   also   acquired
second-hand. It was
one of a pair of Bristol
RELH6G's with ECW,
C47F bodies dating
from 1967. The pair,
UFM   37/9F   (503/4)
were new to Crosville,
another   NBC
subsidiary.

Another second-hand purchase in late 1982 was this 1969 Bristol VRTSL6G with a Gardner engine and ECW H39/31F body. It was one of a pair WHN 411/9G (897/8) acquired for increased school traffic, from United Automobile Services, another NBC subsidiary. After withdrawal in 1986, this bus WHN 411G passed to Silcox of Pembroke Dock for further service.

Accompanied by an ex. West Midlands PTE, Bristol VRT, and an ex. London DMS, at Brunswick Street depot in 1983 is OCD 763G, a Bristol VRT/ECW on loan from Southdown Motor Services. Several buses were hired at this time to cover vehicle shortages, created by upgrading mechanical components on older buses.

PEH 649R was another Bristol VRT with ECW body, on loan in 1983 from Potteries, another NBC subsidiary. It's seen here at the Swansea bus station, working service X1 to Cardiff. Following behind is Lex bodied Bedford YMQS, LCY 298X (298).

London Transport withdrew their DMS class Daimler Fleetlines at a very early age compared to the 'Routemasters'. Thirteen were quickly snapped up by the company in 1983 via Ensign the dealer, who also converted their dual doorway layout to front door and 76 seats. The Fleetlines with Leyland 680 engines and MCW bodies were registered KUC 237/902/924/935/956/991P, TGX 667/853M, GHM 849/880N and KJD 11/19P. KUC 220P was also acquired, but rebuilt to convertible open top. Fleetlines OJD 137/140/144R were also operated 'on hire' from a dealer.

At the time that West Midlands PTE were selling off some of their Bristol VRT's, the company were looking for additional vehicles. Added to the fleet were five ex. West Midlands PTE, Bristol VRT's; NOB 417-9/424M and TOE 434N (902-4/900/1). NOB 415/6M were also acquired and used as driver trainer buses (58/53). They were all fitted with Gardner 6LX engines and MCW, 76 seat high bridge bodies, built to an overall height of 14 feet 2 inches. They were around 12 inches (30cm) higher than the company's ECW bodied VRT's, and regularly sustained damaged roof domes by colliding with low trees, as seen in this photograph of NOB 418M (903).

NOB 416M was one of the two ex. West Midlands PTE, Bristol VRT's mentioned above, acquired for driver training purposes. It's seen here entering Swansea bus station on 21st July, 1987.

A 'surprise' purchase not only for the company, but also for the NBC was that of two Iveco 60-10 mini-coaches in 1985. The 19 seat PSV conversions on both B172/3 BEP (72/3) were carried out by Robin-Hood Coachbuilders. They couldn't be recognized as SWT or NBC vehicles as they only carried the 'Flexibus' branding as shown here on B173 BEP (73) at Sophia Gardens, Cardiff, on 20th February, 1988. 'Flexibus' was only a branding for the private hire fleet, 1985-8.

The first Leyland Olympian double decker's in the fleet arrived in late 1985 as C901-7 FCY (901-7). They were the first 'new' double decker's received in 5 years, and ironically were the last new decker's for the company. Their chassis designation ONCL10/RV indicated that they were fitted with the new Cummins L10 (10 litre) engines, and had Voith automatic transmissions. The bodies built by ECW were to the low height design developed as the successor to the version built on the Bristol VRT chassis. C907 FCY (907) is seen here when quite new on 15th February, 1986, entering Swansea bus station. C903 FCY (903) is also at Swansea Bus Museum awaiting restoration.

Early in 1986, the company took delivery of this superb Duple 425, model SDAK 1503. Integrally built by Duple Coachworks, it seated 49, and was fitted with a toilet. Finished in National Holidays livery, it was numbered 131, and registered 999 BCY, a registration number originally carried by a 1962 AEC Regent V (564). 131 was later re-registered C312 KTH.

Three Plaxton Paramount 4000 double decker coaches were purchased for the 'Rapide' service in 1986, based on the Neoplan 722 chassis. Fitted with the optional Gardner 6LYT (15 litre) engine and automatic transmission, they seated 71 passengers. Numbered 151-3, they were registered SWN159/300CUH/WCY701 respectively, registrations transferred from older company vehicles. 152 is captured here in December 1988, after privatisation of the company.

Another minibus which carried the 'Flexibus' branding was this second - hand Ford Transit SNL 550Y, with a body built by Dormobile seating 16. It's seen here outside the Crown Court at Guildhall Square, Carmarthen, on 28th January, 1987.

In common with other NBC subsidiaries, South Wales Transport commenced urban mini-bus operation in the Swansea area in February 1986. An initial batch of fifteen Mercedes Benz L608D's with conversions to their van body shells carried out by Robin Hood to seat 20, were registered C201-16HTH, (201-16). One of the first batch (203) is seen here at Blaenant Colliery, Crynant, on 29th June, 1989, by then carrying branding 'Cleddau Mini' for Haverfordwest services, but operating a National Coal Board contract from Llanelli depot!

D217 LCY (217) seen here at Cefn Coed Colliery, Crynant, was one of the second batch of Mercedes Benz L608D's delivered in 1986. The view shows an advertisement for private hire, common to all of the company's new mini-buses of that era. The batch, D216-20 LCY (216-20) were fitted with 19 coach type seats, and the remainder, D221-53 LCY (221-53) had 20 bus type seats. This particular bus 217, was a Llanelli depot vehicle carrying the branding of Llanelli services, 'Sosban Link'. The name of 'Sosban' (welsh for saucepan) comes from the strong link the town had with the Llanelli RFC and their anthem 'Sosban Fach'.

Another Llanelli branded vehicle from the same batch as above was D222 LCY (222), but this was fitted with 20 bus seats and a rather unusual roof mounted advertising panel. It's seen here at Market Street, Llanelli, where all the Llanelli town services departed from, from 1986 to March 1997, when a new bus station at Island Place became operational. Island Place bus station has since been redeveloped, housing a Cinema, Theatre, shops and restaurants; the bus station was re-located at adjacent-Stepney Place, constructed with an 'In and Out' facility, not having to reverse the buses. One of this batch, D230 LCY has also found its way into Swansea Bus Museum.

The Mercedes Benz L608D's were ideally suited to work Llanelli local services 182/192 to Morfa in 1986/7, when major road works in the district (re-construction of a sewer) created a diversion under this 9 feet high bridge. The bridge was one of the last two remaining in the district, and as mentioned earlier had necessitated use of specially built AEC Regent V, single decker's in earlier times. The L608D's fitted with advertising 'lids' couldn't operate this route.

Iveco mini-buses didn't appeal to the management of SWT. This Iveco 49-10 with Robin Hood 21 seat conversion operated on loan from the Iveco dealers from 27/9/1986 to 6/10/1986, and is seen here entering Swansea 'Quadrant' bus station on 5th October, 1986.

The first new vehicles purchased by the company after privatisation (a management buy-out on 8th May, 1987) were twenty-five integrally built MCW Metroriders delivered July to September 1987. They were fitted with Cummins B series engines, and had 25 bus seats. Operating services on the west side of Swansea they carried the branding 'City Mini', a name used on mini-buses operating in the Swansea area. D260 PEP (260) was one of three to receive 'D' prefix registrations in July 1987, the remaining twenty-two received 'E' prefix registrations upon delivery a month later. The batch were numbered 254-278.

Only four Mercedes Benz 609's were purchased new by the company. Registered E279-82TTH (279-82), they were new in late 1987, with Robin Hood conversions to their van body shells, seating 20 passengers. They carried the branding 'Valley Link', a name used on Pontardawe based mini-buses, as seen here on 279. All four were sold to Davies Bros, (Pencader) Ltd., in June 1998, but returned to SWT a year later after acquiring the Davies Bros, business.

Within the first year of SWT being privatised, three other companies were absorbed. The first company acquired was the well-established business of AE & FR Brewer, Caerau, in January 1988. A total of thirty-four vehicles of a varied assortment were acquired with the business which had been established in 1921. The Brewers name and licences were retained until 1st April 1998, when Brewers finally merged with SWT in a re-organisation of First Group PLC, to form First Cymru Buses Ltd. One of the vehicles acquired from Brewers in January 1988, was this DAF MB200; C950 GTH with LAG Panoramic C53FT coachwork, which was new to Brewers in January 1986.

MAR 796P (687) was one of many second - hand Leyland National's that were purchased for the Brewers fleet. This one dating from 1976, was identical to the 11.3 meter version's delivered new to SWT between 1973-79. This too was an 11.3 meter 11351A/1R model with B49F layout, and passed to National Welsh in 1991.

There was a large intake of mini-buses into the SWT fleet in 1987-8, amongst them were forty Mercedes Benz 709D's. Delivered as E283-7 UCY, E288-306 VEP, F307-22 AWN (283-322) all were fitted with Reeve Burgess 'Beaver' B25F bodies as shown here by the first of the batch E283 UCY (283), working from Haverfordwest in August, 1989, with the 'Cleddau Mini' branding. They were all re-seated to B23F plus luggage space in 1996/7.

E290 VEP (290), another Mercedes Benz 709D from the 1988 delivery, is seen here at the old Carmarthen bus station on 7th March 1997, working the 131 service to Llanelli, via Meinciau.The service had been inherited on 2nd March, 1997, with the absorption of Davies Bros. (Pencader) Ltd's Trimsaran depot services. The notice on the near-side front window states: 'On hire to Davies Bros.' a legal requirement until the Road Service Licences were transferred.

The 'Flexibus' branding on coaches had been dropped by the time this 1985 Mercedes Benz 608D had been acquired from Winder, Blackpool, in 1988. B993 CHG (74), with a Coachcraft 21 seat conversion to its van derived body shell, was painted into the new coach livery introduced during privatisation in May 1987. In March, 1994, it was re-registered FDZ 985 and re-numbered 274.

Seen here inside Ravenhill depot, Swansea, in March 1989, is this 1982 Leyland Tiger TRCTL11/3R with Duple Goldliner C47FT body, FDZ 982 (182). Originally registered OHM 834Y, it was one of six Tiger's acquired from the Cowie Group, London, in 1988, and is seen here in the National Express livery of that period.

119

Another four Duple 425's were delivered in 1989. Registered F134/5 DEP, and F99/100 CEP (134-7) they had Duple C49FT integral bodies, fitted with the Cummins L10 power unit and automatic transmission. 136/7 were later re-seated to C46FT. F99 CEP (136) seen here at Carmarthen on 19th January, 1991, in the National Express 'Rapide' livery of that period, was on its way to Bournemouth. They were the last 'new' Duple 425's to be purchased.

Ex. London Transport 'Routemaster' VLT 26 (RM 26) was operated on loan to the company from Strathtay Scottish for one week in June 1989, before appearing at the South Wales Transport 75th anniversary celebrations in Margam Country Park. It's seen here at Seven Sisters in the Neath valley, working route 158 to Coelbren, from Neath on 22nd June, 1989.

In May 1989, the company absorbed the Swansea operations of Capitol Coaches, Cwmbran, who operated from the former Morris Bros. depot at Upper Bank. Acquiring Capitol Coaches, together with five coaches became the basis for the formation of 'United Welsh Coaches', and the re-opening of the former United Welsh Services depot (latterly SWT) at Gorseinon, to house the company's United Welsh Coaches fleet. B930 AAX, a 1985 Bedford YNT with Plaxton C53F coachwork is pictured here in August, 1989, still in the Capitol livery, with United Welsh Coaches branding added.

This Duple 425; F100 CEP was delivered in the Brewers livery when new in 1989, carrying fleet number B137, the 'B' indicating 'Brewers'. Built of integral construction with the Cummins L10 engine and automatic transmission, it was designated model number SDA 1512 and had C49FT layout, later re-seated to C46FT.

As mentioned earlier, SWT retained Brewers as a separate company which totally absorbed Llynfi Motor Services at Maesteg in July 1988, with seventeen vehicles. Llynfi operations were then transferred to the Brewers depot at Caerau. Llynfi's licences were discarded along with the fleet-name, but several mini-buses in the fleet appeared with 'Llynfi Mini' branding, a local identity branding for vehicles operating in the Maesteg area. This 1985 Mercedes Benz L608D; C213 PNJ (78), with an Alexander DP20F conversion to its van derived body shell, was acquired from Brighton & Hove in 1990. It was one of the vehicles which carried 'Llynfi Mini' branding.

In 1989, one of the Leyland Leopard's acquired from National Travel (South-West) in 1981, AFH 192T (194) received extensive damage to its Duple Dominant body when it overturned on the M4 Motorway. It's Leyland PSU5C/4R chassis was then re-bodied with this Duple 320, C53F body, and re-registered with cherished number 999 BCY, originally carried by an AEC Regent V, but latterly a Duple 425 integral. 194 was later re-registered AEP 253T and then 278 TNY. It is seen here in the livery of associate company, United Welsh Coaches, on 19th August, 1990.

Working service 11 to Mayhill on the notorious Townhill service, 2nd August, 1989, is this Iveco 49.10 demonstrator, F462 JLG. A good testing ground for any vehicle, with gradients of up to 1 in 5.6 on its 1½ mile climb to 518 feet above sea level! Bodied by Reeve Burgess, it was given 'City Mini' branding and fleet number 362 during its short stay with the company. It's pictured here at Union Street in Swansea.

The Mercedes Benz 709D was a popular choice of mini-bus with the new management of SWT, as a further twenty-two were delivered in 1988. One of the batch, F315 AWN (315) with Reeve Burgess B25F body is seen leaving the old Llanelli bus station at Town Hall Square, for Swansea in 1996. At that time the service ran at 15 minute intervals, with a running time of 55 minutes.

Seen here at Haverfordwest bus station on 14th August, 1993 is another Mercedes Benz 709D from the 1988 delivery. F601 AWN. was one of eight numbered in a different series; F601-8 AWN (601-8). 601-6 were Reeve Burgess B25F, whilst 607/8 had 25, more luxurious high backed dual purpose seats in their standard Reeve Burgess bus body-shells.

As mentioned previously, the business of Brewers, Caerau, was absorbed in January 1988, and six months later Llynfi Motor Services, Maesteg was acquired, followed by Stolzenberg, Maesteg, in June 1990. With the increased activity in that area, the appropriate local branding 'Llynfi Mini' was added to Maesteg based mini-buses, as seen here on F606 AWN (606) in November 1994, re-painted into the Brewers style livery.

The first five Mercedes Benz 811D models were delivered in 1989. The 811D chassis was basically the same as a 709D, but had increased power through a 'turbo-charged' engine. The 811D's purchased in 1989 were F323-7 DCY (323-7) fitted with Reeve-Burgess B25F bodies identical to the earlier 709D's. 325 is seen here when new in 1989, minus it's branding.

In 1989, the mini-buses began to get larger in size. However, no less than fifty-one Mercedes Benz 814D's were delivered in 1989-90 with Robin Hood and Phoenix 31 seat bodies. One of the Robin Hood examples, F337 FCY (337) is seen here working the Carmarthenshire County Council tendered service 194, Llanelli to Carmarthen on a very rural unclassified road between Four Roads and Mynydd-Y-Garreg in February 1999.

Advertising on buses gives bus operators an additional income. This Robin Hood bodied Mercedes Benz 814D, 31 seater, F343 FCY (343) however, received an all over advertisement for Imperial Garages, Haverfordwest in 1990, as seen here in Carmarthen bus station in April 1991.

G347 GEP (347) was numerically the last Robin Hood bodied Mercedes Benz 814D delivered to the company, and is seen here working a Llanelli depot service with Haverfordwest area branding on 2nd May, 1998.

This Mercedes Benz 814D, G365 JTH (365) was one of twenty-seven Phoenix B31F bodied examples delivered in late 1989. It is seen here leaving Haverfordwest bus station for Little Haven on 14th August, 1993, driven by a Llanelli driver, Cedric Glidon, working on loan to Haverfordwest depot.

Pontardawe based mini-buses carried 'Valley Link' branding as seen here on G373 MEP (373) another Phoenix bodied Mercedes Benz 814D from the 1990 delivery.

Two former Mercedes Benz demonstrator vehicles were taken into stock in 1988. The pair of 609D's dating from 1987, were registered D763/4 KWT (363/4), with 20 seat conversions to their van derived bodies by Reeve Burgess and Robin Hood respectively. D764 KWT (364) the Robin Hood example is seen here at Port Talbot bus station carrying the 'Town Mini' branding used by Port Talbot depot.

Updating the coaching side of the business in 1990, the company took delivery of four new Volvo B10M-60's with Plaxton 'Expressliner' C46FT coachwork, for the National Express 'Rapide' network of services. Pictured here at Swansea on 7th March, 1992, is one of the batch, G165 LWN (165), about to depart for Bristol. The batch was registered G164-7 LWN, with matching fleet numbers 164-7.

Not many full sized vehicles operated from the Carmarthen outstation which opened at Johnstown in 1990, but this Leyland National, OEP 795R (795) was one of the few that did. It carried local branding appropriate to the area, 'Bws Myrddin' and also displayed the Dyfed County Council's 'Bws Dyfed' sign, a requirement when operating council tendered services at that time. It was also down-seated to B49F to house a luggage pen, another council requirement.

To operate a new group of Dyfed County Council tendered services in August, 1990, the company placed eight new Mercedes Benz 814D's in service at the new Carmarthen out-station. Registered H374-81 OTH (374-81), they were all bodied by Phoenix as B31F, and branded with the 'Myrddin Mini' logo. Myrddin is a name derived from Caerfyrddin, the welsh name for Carmarthen. H375 OTH (375) is seen here on 19th August 1990, when new.

A pair of 1985, ECW bodied Leyland Olympian double decker coaches were acquired in 1991, from fellow Badgerline subsidiary, Thamesway. Registered B690/6 BPU (908/9), they had long wheel-base chassis; type ONTL11/2RHSp, fitted with standard Leyland TL11 engines, and were coach seated as CH45/28F. Reputedly they were very fast. B696 BPU (909) is seen here in August 1991 working the 'new' Swansea to Cardiff 100 service branded 'Shuttle'. This coach was later re-registered IIL 1829.

Captured here at Tenby on 1ˢᵗ April 1992, is A693 OHJ (170), an Alexander TE bodied Leyland Tiger TRCTL11/2R of 1983. Acquired from Thamesway in 1991, it was one of a batch of six acquired to work in the Brewers fleet and to work the newly acquired 333 limited stop Service, Swansea to Tenby and Pembroke Dock. This tendered service, operated jointly with Davies Bros. (Pencader) Ltd.,was a summertime only service, and lasted two seasons only.

Several Ford Transit mini-buses were acquired from the parent company, Badgerline, Bristol, to work in the Brewers fleet. This particular one, C474 BHY with a Dormobile 16 seat body was previously No 4474 in the fleet of Badgerline at Bristol, and was acquired in 1991.

This Mercedes Benz L608D with a Reeve Burgess B20F body, C478 BHY (222) was also acquired from Badgerline, Bristol in 1991.

Originally numbered B374 in the Brewers fleet, this 1983 Leyland Tiger TRCTL11/2R, with Alexander TE, C53F body, HHJ 374Y was re-numbered 181. It was one of six acquired from Thamesway in 1991. Note the 'Badger' image on the rear-most side panel. This 'Badgerline' emblem was applied to most vehicles in 1993/4.

Another Leyland Tiger TRCTL11/2R with Alexander TE, C49F body acquired from Thamesway in 1991 was A695 OHJ (186), captured here at Bridgend, working the X2 service from Cardiff to Porthcawl.

Many second-hand vehicles were acquired for the Brewers fleet throughout its short existence. Included in the long list was this 1979, 10.3 meter Leyland National type 10351B/1R, 44 seater, XEU 859T (711) which came from the parent company, Badgerline at Bristol in December 1991.

Seen here at Cardiff bus station is yet another vehicle from the Brewers fleet. UAR 598W (598) a Bristol VRT/SL3/6LXB with a standard ECW H43/31F body was acquired from Badgerline group company; Eastern National, (3108), in April 1992. It was later re-numbered 949, to make-way for incoming Dennis Darts 581-599.

Another vehicle seen displaying the Badgerline logo – the Badger, is K407 BAX (407) from the batch of ten Mercedes Benz 811D's (401-10) delivered to Brewers in March 1993. They were all fitted with Plaxton 'Beaver', B31F bodies.

SWT acquired this 1994 Wadham-Stringer bodied Mercedes Benz 811D from Pullman Coaches of Crofty, in December 1995, with the Swansea Rail-link contract. By the time this view was taken on 23rd March, 1996, the contract had finished, yet the vehicle was still carrying Rail-Link livery, with new branding for the Time-cutter X75 service Swansea to Merthyr and Aberdare. Acquired as a 33 seater, the company wasted no time in down- seating it to B31F, to comply with SWT's own agreement, that a driver would be paid an enhanced rate of pay to drive a vehicle with more than 31 seats.

Cherished registration number J1 SWT was fitted to this Volvo B10M-60 from new in 1991. Fitted with Plaxton Expressliner coachwork, it seated 46 and had the usual National Express 'Rapide' facilities. Seen here at Carmarthen on 26th October, 1991, it was one of five Volvo B10M's delivered as J1-5 SWT (101-5) in 1991/2, the latter four being Expressliner 2's.101, seen here was re-registered J495 WEP before sale in 1996.

Seen here when new in June 1994 is L601 FKG (601), a 9.8 meter, Plaxton B40F bodied Dennis Dart. It was one of eight, L601-8 FKG (601-8) delivered for the 'Brewers' fleet. The Brewers Darts had larger seating capacities compared to SWT, as the 31 seat rule for rates of pay didn't apply to Brewers and United Welsh staff. The 'Badger' logo fitted to the rear most side panel became standard practice on new deliveries to all Badgerline companies from 1993 onwards.

Only one Volvo B10M-60, was purchased in 1993. L506 GEP (106), a Plaxton Expressliner 2, with C46FT layout, was that vehicle, and is seen here at Carmarthen bus station working service 708 to Birmingham on 27th January, 1994. The Expressliner 2, was based on the Premier design and had some incorporating features to meet National Express requirements.

A major intake of new buses by the company in 1993 included the first order for 24 Dennis Darts with Plaxton Pointer, 9 meter bodies, all seating 31. These buses were capable of seating 36, but were down-seated in order to comply with a local wage agreement – mini bus drivers rate of pay. Over 31 seats fitted, warranted 'conventional bus' rate of pay. L515 HCY (515) seen here with 'City Mini' branding was one of the first batch L501-24 HCY (501-24) delivered in 1993. Numerically the first of the batch, L501 HCY (501) is now in preservation at the Swansea Bus Museum.

The 1994 delivery of new Dennis Darts was for another twenty-six identical 9 meter, Plaxton bodied 31 seaters, which were registered L525-50 JEP (525-50). L531 JEP (531), is seen here at Swansea, in 'City Mini' livery, working service 36, which was branded 'Pink Route' at that time. All the major Swansea routes were branded with colour codes in 1993!

Switching from Volvo, the company's first Dennis Javelin coaches arrived in late 1994, for the National Express 'Rapide' network of services. Registered M107/8 NEP (107/8), they had Plaxton Expressliner 2, bodies, finished in full National Express 'Rapide' requirements. Three more were delivered in early1995.

Dennis Javelin, M108 NEP (108) seen here with a Plaxton Expressliner 2, body, quickly received a re-paint into the new National Express 'Air Link' livery as shown in this view taken on 29th July, 1995.

No less than nineteen of these 1986 Mercedes Benz L608D's with Dormobile B20F, conversions were transferred from Bristol City Line, (a Badgerline company) into the SWT and Brewers fleets between 1994/5. They were used for a variety of services including the Landore Park & Ride in Swansea, which was only £1.00 in December 1994.

On the 16th June 1995, Badgerline merged with Grampian Regional Transport, forming First Bus PLC. Retaining the SWT identity after the merger, the company received its first batch of new Dennis Dart buses. There was no outwardly difference with these buses apart from the Badger logos' were replaced by a First Bus ' f ' logo in the rear window. The batch of seven-teen Plaxton Pointer, bodied 31 seater, Dennis Dart's: N551-9/61-8 UCY (551-9/61-8), were the last new step entrance Darts delivered to SWT in late 1995. They were all 9 meter versions. From that batch, 563 is seen in January 1996 working service 4, a service now operated by 'FTR' Bendy-buses.

On 6th January 1996, SWT, (by now controlled by First Bus PLC) acquired the business of Rees & Williams, at Tycroes, which was part of the 'D' Coaches, Morriston group of companies. The Tycroes depot was also acquired together with nine buses and all stage carriage services. L364 GTH (384), a Mercedes Benz 609D seen here was one of the vehicles acquired with the business, and is noteworthy in being the first of the type converted to PCV specification by Cymric Conversions of Kidwelly.

The Rees & Williams fleet-name continued to be used by the company until the vehicles bearing that name were disposed of. H853 OWN (386), a 1990 Mercedes Benz 811D with automatic transmission and Reeve Burgess 'Beaver' B31F body was another vehicle acquired from the Rees & Williams take-over in January 1996.

Five 9.8 meter Dennis Dart's were acquired with the merger of Rees & Williams' business in 1996. J580 VTH (397) seen here, was numerically the first, and had a Plaxton Pointer 40 seat body, putting it into the category of 'conventional bus' drivers rate of pay, even though numbered into the mini-bus fleet number series. It's seen here at Carmarthen bus station, 8th March, 1997, just before work commenced to re-develop the bus station in April that year.

K82 BWN (399) was another former Rees & Williams 9.8 meter Dennis Dart, but this one had an Alexander Dash, B40F body, and dated from 1992. It's captured here on 5th February, 1999, working the short lived Llanelli to Carmarthen 'tendered' 194 service. The location of this very rural scene is an unclassified single track road between Four Roads and Mynydd-Y-Garreg.

Several elderly Leyland Nationals' taken into stock in January 1996 to work the Rees & Williams services. YEV 311S (1853), a Leyland National, type 11351A/1R, seen here on 6th January, 1996, at Ammanford bus station, originated from Eastern National (1853), and was acquired to cover vehicle shortages at Rees & Williams in the interim period. It retained this livery and fleet number with SWT, but carried Rees & Williams fleet-names, and SWT operator licence.

Another Brewers vehicle seen at Cardiff bus station is this Leyland Tiger TRBTL11/2R, with Duple Dominant DP47F body. Registered A658 KUM it carried fleet number (164) and was acquired from Yorkshire Rider in March 1996.

AAX 450A (853), a 1983 Leyland Tiger TRCTL11/3R, with Plaxton Paramount 3200, C51F body, was new to National Welsh as SDW 914Y. Acquired by Red & White Services, Cwmbran in 1991, it passed to SWT (First Group) with four others in 1996 to cover the vehicle shortage at Tycroes depot after the merger of Rees & Williams. It's pictured here on the 4th October, 1998 with 'Cymru' branding, but still licenced to South Wales Transport!

Transferred to SWT (First Group) from Provincial (First Group) Hampshire in 1998, was this 1991 Mercedes Benz 811D, fitted with automatic transmission and Carlyle B29F body. H173 GTA (451) was one of four based at Llanelli depot, and is seen here working the 196 Llanelli to Carmarthen service on 7th March, 1999. This service was taken over from Davies Bros (Pencader) Ltd., in March 1997 – the first part of the Davies Bros' take-over.

Acquired from Western National O.C. (709) in March 1996, for the company's Brewers fleet, was this 1991 Mercedes Benz 709D, 21 seater. J901 MAF (429) was new to a Cornish operator; Ede,of Par, and was originally registered J6 EDE; the operators name! It's seen here working the Carmarthenshire C.C. tendered 194 service between Mynydd-y-Garreg and Four Roads in 1999.

The first vehicles delivered in the new First Group 'barbie' livery were registered R581-99 SWN (581-99). They were Dennis Dart SLF's, with Plaxton Pointer bodies, and still carried SOUTH WALES TRANSPORT legal lettering and operator licence discs: so were 'legally' still SWT! Numerically first of the batch, 581 is seen here soon after delivery, at the Transport Festival, Singleton Park, Swansea on 4th May 1998, demonstrating the low floor access and displaying the new livery.

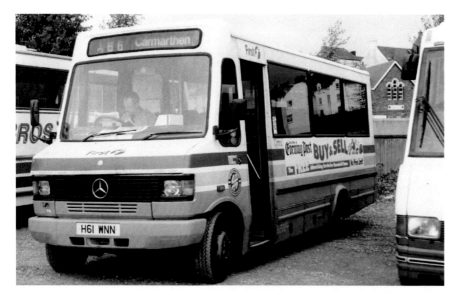

The final part of Davies Bros.(Pencader) Ltd., was absorbed in June 1999, with the purchase of their Carmarthen depot, school contracts and remaining services, together with 39 vehicles. The Private Hire, Holidays and Tours side of Davies Bros. was not acquired. Taking into consideration that the new 'barbie' livery had been introduced over a year earlier, the Davies Bros. vehicles were repainted into the SWT livery of leaf green, lime green and white with red relief, as shown here on H61 WNN (273), a Mercedes Benz 709D with Scott, DP29F body.

A very interesting vehicle acquired with the Davies Bros. takeover was this Leyland Tiger, TRCTL11/3ARZ. The chassis was built in 1984 as a development and experimental chassis, and used for testing any modification before putting it in to production - so was an 'up to date' model. It was bought by Davies Bros at the Leyland Motors closing down sale in June 1991. Sent to Plaxton's in 1992 for bodying, it was the last Leyland Tiger to be fitted with a new Plaxton Paramount 3200 body in October 1992, and seated 57. Due to its chassis age, DVLA gave it an age related registration number: A171 UDE, but unhappy J.D.Davies immediately re-registered it with this cherished number, 2358 DD. 2358 DD = Dewi Davies! (MD).

ADU 327X (155), a 1981 Leyland Tiger TRCTL11/3R, with Plaxton Supreme V, C57F coachwork was showing signs of its age here when it was acquired with the Davies Bros business in 1999, (18 years old) and was soon disposed of. It's captured here leaving the new Carmarthen bus station on 27th October 1999, still in Davies Bros' livery, carrying SWT fleet number 155.

5210 DD (143) was new to Davies Bros. in August 1988 as F614 RBX. It was another Leyland Tiger, but was powered with a Cummins L10 engine, and designated chassis type TRCL10/3ARZM, fitted with a Plaxton Paramount 3500 body to C51FT layout. It was given fleet number 143 by the company and re-painted into SWT's green, white and red livery.

This Duple 340 bodied Leyland Tiger, 8853 DD (146) was also new to Davies Bros., in March 1988 as E237 MBX (168). It was one of the first Leyland Tiger's built with a Cummins L10 engine, (chassis no.TR0005) and had a 7 speed ZF manual gearbox. Its seen here soon after its re-paint into SWT livery.

137

Another Leyland Tiger TRCL10/3ARZM with Plaxton Paramount 3200, C53F coachwork acquired from Davies Bros, was 6690 DD. New in 1988, and originally registered F721 ENE, it was one of a pair Davies Bros. purchased from Shearing's Holidays, Wigan, in April 1995. This was given fleet number 151 by the company.

M256 CDE (393) was one of six Mercedes Benz 811's taken over from Davies Bros., in June 1999, registered M253-8 CDE (390-3/7/8). All six were bodied by Mellor Coachworks in 1994 to B31F layout.

Davies Bros., had operated a large fleet of Leyland Leopard's, but only four were taken into stock with the business. Seen here at Carmarthen depot is GCY 124W (711), a Leopard PSU3E/4R, with Plaxton Supreme Express IV, C53F body, which had carried cherished registration number FEK 1 F when acquired by SWT. GCY 124W was new to Creamline, Tonmawr, in 1980.

COMPANY PREMISES

The engineering shop when it was housed at Brunswick Street Garage in the early 1930's.

Eastland Road garage, Neath was built on premises acquired from Neath Corporation in 1933, replacing an earlier smaller garage in London Road, Neath. Thirty-three buses were housed in this depot which closed in 1972 after the United Welsh and Western Welsh depots were acquired, which led to concentration on the former Western Welsh depot at Neath.

A selection of vehicles housed at Brunswick Street Garage, Swansea, in 1951, included these AEC Regal lll's, and Regent lll's of 1950/1, and Leyland Titan TD7's of 1939.

Ravenhill Works was built in 1937, arising from the major expansion of the company's fleet, needed to replace the Swansea tramway system (S.I.T.C.). This view was taken around 1950.

The Central Works section of Ravenhill Garage in 1954.

Ravenhill Garage, Penlan, Swansea, as it was in 1954.

The interior of Ravenhill Garage, Penlan, Swansea in 1958. It was built in 1936/7, and could house 140 vehicles, all under cover, in a structure that was free of centre supports.

The company constructed this garage in Copperworks Road, Llanelli, to house the entire fleet allocated to Llanelli. The floor space of this building was free of structural pillars, and built in 1938. Previously, the fleet had been kept at Spring Gardens and Mina Street, Llanelli, and maintained in their garage at Erw Road, Llanelli, a site now occupied by Avenue Villa Surgery. Following the take-over of Llanelly & District Traction Co., the trolleybus undertaking in 1952, both depots were used. In 1964 it was decided to house everything at the former trolleybus depot in Robinson Street, the older of the two depots. Copperworks Road depot was then closed in 1964, and sold to the lessor; Neville Druce & Co., The Copperworks, Llanelli, for storage purposes.

This premises at Plymouth Street, Swansea was acquired in September 1945, for use as an enquiry office and booking office for extended tours and day excursions. It was leased from Worthington & Co. Ltd, the Brewers. This office was virtually on the doorstep of their competitors, United Welsh Services' new Coach Station.

A view of Russell Street offices, Swansea showing part of Brunswick Street, where the company's first garage was situated.

The land for this garage at Pontardawe was acquired in 1928 to cater for the company's rapidly expanding services in the Swansea Valley. The 728 sq. yard plot of land cost £1,323 and the cost of erecting the garage in 1928, which housed nine-teen vehicles was £2,762. This picture was taken in 1950.

(Below)
The new garage at Pontardawe photographed in 1960.

The interior of Ammanford garage and bus station, as acquired in 1962, from James of Ammanford.

The 'Coach Station' at Singleton Street, Swansea was acquired with the merger of United Welsh Services Ltd., in 1970/1.
It had an imposing frontage on to Singleton St., which was the passenger entrance. Buses entered from Plymouth St., and
left by the exit doors on the other side of the building leading into Princess St. (on the right of the picture).
Keeping its original façade, the building has since been renovated and changed into a retail store for Wilkinsons!

The former United Welsh Services garage here at Clarence Terrace, Swansea was also acquired in the merger of United Welsh in 1970/1.

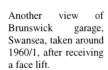Another view of Brunswick garage, Swansea, taken around 1960/1, after receiving a face lift.

During the fuel shortages of World War 2, many buses were converted to run on gas, and therefore towed a trailer carrying a gas producer, as seen in this photograph. The vehicle in this instance is AEC Regent, ACY 23 (224), a bus which received extensive damage in a fatal accident in 1943, when it overturned down an embankment, landing on its roof on top of several railway trucks.

ANCILLARY VEHICLES

This AEC Matador breakdown and recovery lorry was used in the 1960's. The body structure was far more modern than it's chassis.

When this AEC Regent III, FWN 353 (315) was withdrawn from passenger service in 1962, it had its roof removed as seen in this photograph. It was then given a new lease of life and used as a driver trainer – in this condition until it was sold for scrap in 1968. The other trainer vehicle visible is FWN 354 (316)

This AEC Regent III tree lopper was also converted from a 1949 Weymann bodied double decker; FWN 361 (323) in 1961, and remained as such until 1968, when it was sold for scrap.

The company had a
varied assortment of
breakdown and
recovery vehicles
throughout its history,
but this Magirus-
Deutz had to be the
best recovery vehicle
of them all. It's
captured here at
Fforestfach in June
1981, giving a
suspended tow to
Leyland National,
AWN 810V (810).

Another view of the
Magirus – Deutz recovery
vehicle was taken on the
Gower Peninsular during
the bad winter of 1988-9.
By this time it had been
registered Q953 TEP, not
allowed to run on trade
plates anymore.

The very last recovery
vehicle purchased by the
company in 1996 was this
Bedford TM, with a General
Motors (GM) 'Detroit' V6
engine. It had spent
most of its working life as
an articulated tractor unit
with Vauxhall Motors,
Luton, towing a car
transporter trailer. It was
acquired from
Davies Bros. (Pencader)
Ltd., who had used it as a
tow truck since 1988 -- in
exchange for a Leyland
Leopard, NMS 564M.
However, SWT modified
the lorry by lengthening its
chassis and fitting the
recovery crane.

146

TICKETS USED

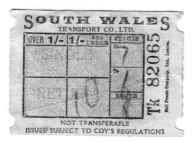
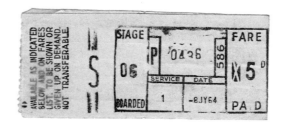